Where Have You Gone, Lance Alworth?

Stories About Growing Up in Arkansas

by

Grady Jim Robinson

To Carol

To a lady who adored a real Hero.

From Grady Jim R...

Diamond Gem Publishing
Fayetteville, Arkansas
www.GradyJim.com

ISBN: 0-9638832-1-6
Diamond Gem Publishing
Fayetteville, Arkansas

Cover design by Vulcan Creative Labs.
www.vulcancreative.com
Cover art by Jared Lee.

For Ryan

A perfect baby, a wonderful boy and a fine scholar
who has his father's total blessing.

Acknowledgments

Dozens of people have read these stories during the past ten years and have commented on them. I can't remember them all. But I want to thank several people who were especially helpful. Thanks to Evangeline Eysmael of Phoenix, Ariz., who spent a lot of hours reading, typing and commenting on my attempts to tell my story.

I want to thank Linda Verigan at *Sports Illustrated* who found "The Diving Contest" in a pile of unsolicited manuscripts in 1979 and published that story in the magazine. It was immediately picked up by *Reader's Digest* and appeared in October of 1979. The success of that story opened the way for 26 more stories in *SI*.

I must thank Brad Summerhill of the Creative Writing Program at the University of Arkansas who gave professional feedback. Thanks also go to volunteer readers Rita Risser and Irene Stemler of the National Speakers Association. A special thank you to the members of the National Speakers Association, my storytelling community for 20 years, for encouragement in the long development of these stories in oral form.

Jane Seagraves of St. Louis, my devoted assistant and friend for 10 years, typed and retyped many of these stories a dozen times. She was always supportive and encouraging even when she secretly hoped I'd finally finish with the re-writing. Thanks also to high school friend Pam Curry of Fayetteville.

Thank you to Steve Wright of Ozark Delta Press in Fayetteville who passed along invaluable publishing and marketing advice.

A very special thank you goes to the Angel of Dickson Street, Stephanie Meehan. When I moved back to Arkansas and found Stephanie in her office at EdiType, I knew it was just a matter of time before I would have these stories in the best shape possible for this collection. Stephanie is a true professional who does far more than typing and editing. She has exceptional skills in the use of the computer to file, re-file and update files. But it's far more than mechanical skill that makes her so special. She always worked with such good grace and supported me with charm, patience, gentle guidance when needed, lots of good humor and sometimes just the right touch of sarcasm.

A loving thank you to Janita Cooper of Master Duplicating in Phoenix who has been an uncommon friend during recent times of crisis in my life.

Without the unconditional love, spiritual guidance, unceasing encouragement and full blessing of my twenty-year soulmate, Rosita Perez of Gainesville, Florida, this book would not have been completed.

CONTENTS

Introduction

Storytelling is an ancient and honorable profession. Way back in caveperson days the tribe gathered around the fire at night, ate bear meat and told tales about the day's adventures. Naturally certain individuals became more proficient at storytelling than others. Before too long those who could tell the best story about the hunt were more powerful in the tribe than those who could actually hunt — which eventually led to lawyers and politicians.

We assume that certain storytellers began to embellish the stories to make them better which led to the epic story such as *Beowulf,* which led to novels like *Moby Dick* and then later movies such as *Star Wars*.

The famous philosopher Jean-Paul Sartre once said,"We understand everything through story." Our life is understood through the stories we tell about our experiences, individually, as a community or culture and as a race of people.

The stories I tell about my experiences are probably more entertaining than the actual experiences themselves. People have said to me from time to time, "You sure had an interesting childhood." In reality it was fairly normal. I admit to having a strong interest in stories about my experiences.

Psychologists tell us that we attempt to understand our life through the stories we choose to tell, "choose to tell" being the key phrase. I recall many events that I choose not to tell. Those events are not a part of what I want to remember about myself. Furthermore, we attempt to justify our life and what we have become by creating stories about our childhood that may or may not be true in the historical sense. Dr. James Hillman has addressed this important issue in his book, *The Soul's Code.* Hillman points out that such notable individuals as John Wayne, Ronald Reagan and Henry Ford created stories about their own childhood experiences that other family members found impossible to believe. Henry Ford used to tell everyone that he worked on watches as a boy and that he had a small watch maker's table covered with watches. He claimed to have actually stolen watches from neighbors' homes and worked on them. As an adult he restored his childhood home and placed a watch maker's table covered with watches in his old room. His sister said she had never noticed the table and to her recollection young Henry had no special interest in watches and certainly not those of the neighbors. Hillman includes dozens of other examples of adults re-structuring their childhood to fill some kind of need as an adult.

My own need to tell stories about my childhood is likely some kind of subconscious attempt to justify or explain who and what I have become.

Lance Alworth was a sports hero who later became a symbol of greatness, athletic prowess, fame and even took on a kind of mystery. He was my Elvis and Superman all rolled into one Razorback football player. He was everything I wanted to be. Growing up in the home of a football coach it was natural that football became the metaphor through which I would view my early life. When I stood on the sidelines as a six-year-old boy watching my father coach football I stood at his feet and gazed upward to see grown men wearing armor, covered with sweat, dirt, blood, war wounds, gasping for air, warriors in the midst of combat. It naturally became my view of manhood.

The high school players of the early and mid-fifties such as Homer Dyer, Jimmy Griffin and Tommy Blair became heroes and even more importantly, symbols. And if these, my heroes, worked hard to earn the respect and approval of MY father, then how much more so should I earn his approval.

In 1957 when I was in junior high school, Alworth arrived from Mississippi to play for the Arkansas Razorbacks under coach Frank Broyles. To me Lance Alworth was a god.

Down deep in my soul was a writer, storyteller and a comedian, but those traits were not valued in Greenwood, Arkansas, in those days. Football and baseball were valued and were the activities through which a young man would establish his place in the pecking order of playground rivalry. My true self, the future storyteller, was at odds with what I felt I must become, a superstar athlete, a ballplayer, a warrior.

In the sixth grade many of the boys played football at recess, or what we called "run through tackle." Later I learned this game was known in other parts of the country as "kill the guy with the ball." I recall Bud Needham, by far the toughest kid in our class, scooping up the football and running like a madman for the far end of the playground with two dozen boys in pursuit. He would tear through the middle of them and stiff-arm a kid in the face, slam headlong into an innocent victim who happened to get in the way and tear shirts to shreds as he stormed through the screaming mob. I carefully avoided those games of "run through tackle" and hung out with the girls around the monkey bars. About 45 years later I found myself in a game of tackle football at the age of 53 with my son's college friends on the lawn at Boston College.

That experience led to the first story in this collection, "Where Have You Gone, Lance Alworth?"

But when we entered the seventh grade I was first in line to get my uniform and declare that I was a football player. I played in junior high which led to one of my best stories in *Ford Times* magazine. It was published under the title "The Day We Tackled Billy Bob Burkette." In this collection I changed the name of the runner to his real name, Bobby Joe Needham. Yes, Bud Needham's older brother.

I had other heroes at that time. Stan Musial, the St. Louis Cardinal outfielder who won seven batting titles. On May 2, 1954, Stan The Man hit five home runs. I have included that story which first appeared in *Sports Illustrated* in this collection.

I desperately wanted to earn my spurs in the arena that our culture and our community had chosen. But I am now convinced that I was ill-suited for that role. Strangely enough one of the stories in this collection is called "Thanksgiving Day Football," and it is the true tale of redemption on the field.

Childhood stories and ancient myth often have parallels. Most of the great writers including Hemingway, Faulkner, McMurtry, Joyce, Fitzgerald, Burroughs, and on and on, had very serious Oedipal issues that were lifelong undercurrents in their work. I don't compare myself to those great writers. They continued to write about their fathers throughout their career, and they dealt with bouts of depression all their lives. Psychologist Kay Redfield Jamison has linked the desire to write (or retell one's story), bouts of depression, and unresolved Oedipal issues in these famous writers.

With both my mother and father in education it is still somewhat of a mystery why I struggled with school. From the first day of school, which I remember as if it were yesterday, I felt lost, bewildered, out of focus and nervous. I don't know why.

By the second grade it was very clear that I was not a good student. When Mrs. Bell placed me in the Canary reading group I knew I was doomed. It's a true story. All the smart kids were in the Redbirds or Bluebirds. A few of the more "challenged" were in the Robins. I was in the Canary reading group with another kid who shall remain nameless.

I've spent the rest of my life reading, writing and telling stories one of which is about being in the Canary reading group. I don't know what that means but it must mean something really deep. I've made a lot of money telling that Canary reader story to education groups. I call the oral version of that story "The Revenge of the Canary Reader."

In the seventh grade I thought I might be a rock and roll star, thus the first and only performance of the Jazz Kittenz. It was truly pitiful. Can you imagine four seventh graders in front of the whole school to play "Rock Around The Clock?"

Thank God for Wilma. Women who knew her and worked with her at the elementary school for decades tell me to this day that she was blessed with sensitivity, wit, love for children and joy in teaching. She seemed to understand my struggle. She saw that I was overly sensitive, overly emotional (still am), and trying desperately to be the Lance Alworth that I thought would please my father and compete with my older brother. She tried to steer me in another direction with subtle and sometimes very witty comments and suggestions. "James, you're the funniest kid around," she would say.

I had a wonderful childhood with great parents and family in a truly wonderful little town in Arkansas. There is no explanation as to why I seemed to struggle with my own inner demons far more than most kids.

Recently I was inducted into the National Speakers Hall of Fame to stand beside such venerable orators as Norman Vincent Peale, Ronald Reagan, Art Linkletter and Zig Ziglar.

I got a little teary eyed thinking about my father and how surprised he would be.

I hope you find joy, and perhaps some healing, as you read, "Where Have You Gone, Lance Alworth?"

Grady Jim Robinson
Fayetteville, Arkansas

PART I
Childhood

Where Have You Gone, Lance Alworth?

I guess it was pretty silly for a guy who now measures time by the number of decades since Lance Alworth was a Razorback to be standing on a football field awaiting a kickoff. Somehow I didn't feel 53 years old standing there in wet grass, barefoot, assuming the game I'd gotten in with my son's Boston College schoolmates was touch football. It seemed like a mere flick of time, a quick handoff, a 60-yard dash, one long bomb, a snappy half-a-century since that day in 1959 I slipped by security and sat beside my ultimate hero, Lance Bambi Alworth (No. 23), on the Arkansas bench. Bambi was everything I wanted to be: a football star, famous, mystical, bigger than life. He was my DiMaggio, Ruth, Musial all rolled into one Arkansas Razorback.

I wasn't much of a "hitter" even as a kid although I loved the running and throwing part of football. If I'd known it was going to be tackle without padding or even shoes, it would have taken much more inducement to get me on the field. But there I was.

Apparently college kids don't play touch or flag football these days. My son, Ryan (psychology major '99), was lined up to play. Most were members of the BC marching band and there was even a girl. Did I say, "even a girl" as if I were stunned? Yes, I admit it. I did. I was stunned that a girl was about to play in a game of tackle. Fifty years ago you just didn't find a girl out on the field playing football. This mindset from decades past would come back to haunt me.

"C'mon, Pops, you gotta play! We need your body," Ryan had yelled from the field.

"Ryan, I'm too old for football."

"C'mon, Pops. We won't hurt you."

So there I stood awaiting the kickoff assuming I was nimble enough to at least stay out of the way in this game of *touch football.*

I had not sprinted since lime-green leisure suits were the rage, which means, come to think of it, before most of these guys and gals were in diapers. They're Echo-Boomers. Our kids. They've never heard of bell bottoms. A party line means something entirely different to them. They never feared polio.

They love McGwire but they never saw Mantle.

They love Elway but don't know Unitas.

They love Jordan but probably don't remember Baylor.

Where have you gone, Lance Alworth?

"Just touch on the kickoff," someone yelled. This was my first indication it might be a game of real tackle football.

You don't walk off the field just because it's tackle, even at my age, so I thought, well hell, maybe I can throw a pass like high school days just 36 seasons ago.

Ryan played across from me. I whispered as we lined up after the kickoff. "Ryan, we're not playing real tackle are we?"

"Sure, Pop, and I'm coming right over your butt," he snarled.

I hiked the ball, watched it wobble toward our thrower, then looked up to block my own son who weighs 250 pounds but he was already by me heading for the quarterback. I grabbed his shirt and hung on. He pulled me across the wet grass like I was water skiing.

Bodies flew through the air with sounds of flesh slapping flesh, bodies crashing to the ground, t-shirts ripping apart as strong hands grabbed for the frantic runner who ran for his life. I had not heard such snorts and grunts and thuds and yelps since we tried to tackle Bud Needham in the sixth grade. I attempted to stay out of the way. It reminded me why I had been such a mediocre football player in high school. Because my father, whom I adored, was the coach, I felt guilty that I was not a mean linebacker, or maybe a Bambi-like halfback on the high school team. For almost four decades I suppressed feelings of inadequacy about high school football. As an adult I became a writer, storyteller and comedian. It didn't require Freud to notice that most of my stories were about childhood attempts to earn the blessing and love of my father.

It soon became obvious these BC band members were terribly serious about playing football. I had lost touch with the physical power and desire to compete in young men, and women, as we shall soon see. A particular young man, thickly built, made several violent runs through our entire team before being dragged down; Michael Quinn is a philosophy major from Cleveland who, I learned later, longs to be a priest, a philosophy teacher or perhaps a mystic. He's a strong young man who, when not reading Hildergard of Bengin, enjoys weight lifting — bench pressing around 250 pounds — and tossing his body helter-skelter through mid-air at unfortunate french horn players carrying footballs.

I snapped the ball and tiptoed away from the violence watching them smack bodies together and gang tackle the future father, Quinn, dubbed very quickly "The Diesel." On defense I banged at Ryan and chased the thrower.

When Alworth was a Razorback, girls didn't play football. Today, thanks to Gloria Steinem, Billy Jean King and Title IX, when college kids play their Saturday afternoon football game it doesn't faze the boys that a girl wants to play. Holly Sheldon from Long Island, NY, a trumpet player in the Eagle marching band, caught a pass, sprinted down field and was floored by two guys who did not smirk, smile or apologize when they got up off of her. Then she caught another one and another one and each time was blasted just like the guys with no mention of the fact she was a girl. This is a generational shift and you young people are going to have to let us old people marvel at this. Then she caught a pass at the five-yard line. As I stood and watched, she stiff-armed a would-be tackler and before my very eyes lowered her right shoulder and, like Jim Brown, with ponytail bouncing slammed through two guys into the endzone. All I could do was just stand there with my mouth open and think, "This ain't 1959!"

They slapped high fives and jogged up the field for the kickoff.

That must have got my adrenaline going or made me forget the 36 years since high school football. On the next series of downs I moved out to wide receiver and lined up just like Lance Alworth. Bambi, we called him four decades ago. The lightfooted boy from Jackson, Mississippi, ran a 9.6 hundred, was a Razorback All-American, San Diego Charger All-Pro, leading receiver in the AFL, unanimous Hall of Famer, and just five years ago voted the greatest wide receiver in professional football.

You young people think Jerry Rice can run? You think Randy Moss can shake and bake? Alworth played wide receiver like Louie Armstrong played jazz. There were two other things about Alworth that allowed him to transcend athletic stardom. Two factors that made him dream-like, beyond the realm of mere mortals. Lance was blessed with movie star good looks. He possessed big Bambi-like eyes, a pouting lip, perfect cheekbones. He was Elvis in cleats. He also ran on his toes and pranced like a trained trotting horse with high knee lift and rhythmic shoulder swing that translated to visual poetry. A Picasso in Razorback red.

With fantasies of the Great Bambi in my head, I lumbered forward on the snap and broke inside and waved my arms but our quarterback was already in a mad scramble for his life fleeing the mystic from Cleveland who appeared to be thinking mayhem, not mysticism.

Suddenly the ball was wobbling toward me and I thought, Where is the Diesel? I caught and sprinted for the sideline hoping to get out of bounds soon. I lumbered onward toward safety. Nations rose and fell. Then I felt a hard thud from behind along with the faintest whiff of perfume and my 53-year-old butt bounced off the hard ground. A five-yard completion. It felt strange to be tackled for the first time in more than three decades. But I could only laugh and with some pride accept a hand up from the apologetic tackler, Holly "The Hit Woman" Sheldon.

Ryan yelled across the field with some concern in his voice, "You all right, Pops?"

"I think so!" I said laughing as the boys slapped high fives for the old gamer.

Then it happened.

The boys paid little attention to Ryan's old man. They didn't know he had speed to burn stored for decades in aged legs that once covered 100 yards in 9.8 seconds in the 1966 Oklahoma AAU meet in Shawnee, Oklahoma

I had to go for it. Bambi lived in my mind and heart if not my legs. After all those years of nightmares about my perceived failure to gain the respect of my father-coach, perhaps I could make it happen.

Maybe I could finally be Lance Alworth, not for my long-dead father but for my son.

The QB looked over his offense. I caught his eye and motioned my head downfield. Going deep. The quarterback, who possessed a powerful arm for a trombone player, called the signals.

The ball was snapped.

I exploded from the line of scrimmage. OK, I didn't explode. I eased out slowly so as not to excite the defense nor alarm my hamstring muscles. I was running downfield.

Horrors! I looked up to see the future mystic thundering my way apparently having seen my signal. The look on his face was the kind you get by reading too much Nietzsche at a young age.

What in God's name, I said to myself, am I doing here? It's perfectly legal for him to break me in half. It's real football we're playing here. He's serious about his Saturday afternoon football game. He's focused on that one moment during the week when a young man may, through the legal violence of football, rid himself of excess testosterone built up by vigorous weight lifting, philosophical studies and self-imposed priestly denials of the normal outlets.

I probably should have simply pulled up.

But no! The old man has some testosterone left. The old stag against the young buck. The typewriter vs. email. Black Converse high tops vs. Air Jordans.

In memory of the nickel coke, dime fries, Buddy Holly, Patsy Cline, Huntley-Brinkley, Ed Sullivan, Cassius Clay, and the greatest athletic dancer of all time, Lance Bambi Alworth, I fly onward.

Recalling my own competitive days of yore, I run, flying almost weightless at high speed across the grass, knees pumping like pistons, trusting what little hamstring fiber hopefully remained from of all those workouts on the wind swept, red dirt of Oklahoma. Hearing the sound of heavy breathing and the pounding steps of the weight-lifting mystic intent on annihilation, I turn to see a spiraling football high above the field with the nose twirling perfectly. Instant calculations seem to indicate that the ball and I — assuming a leg did not suddenly knot up and wrap itself around my neck — will arrive at the same spot downfield at exactly the same moment.

I ran down the field that day knowing that my son was watching his old man. My football coach father had been dead for 20 years, and it was too late to show him how great I could be, barefoot, like flying in those recurring dreams I'd had for forty years, above the football field, flying, turning loops.

The ball zeroed in toward my stomach much like a smartbomb; Montana to Rice, Unitas to Berry, Meredith to Hayes, Staubach to Pearson, Bradshaw to Swann, Griese to Warfield, Hadl to Alworth and, of course, Flutie to Phelan.

The trombone player to Ryan's old man.

Earth ceased its revolutions, rivers stopped running to the sea, armies ceased marching, glaciers stopped melting, babies stopped crying, lawyers stopped lying, birds stopped singing, bells stopped ringing, and decades vanished as the pigskin descended.

Right in the breadbasket. The old man clutched the ball. End zone. Touchdown.

"Ryan's old man, M-V-P!!" They chanted, laughed and high fived.

I jot these notes in Mod 6A as Ryan moves his books in for his senior year at BC. I sip a rum and coke with a splash of aspirin. We're going out to eat later if I can get up.

I wonder if Old Bambi can still go deep. Has it really been four decades? He dances still in my dreams. Where have you gone, Lance Alworth?

The Farm

There was an old man sitting in a rocking chair by a black iron stove with a coal fire inside. The room was hot and filled with smoke. I was standing in the kitchen door looking at the old man. Mama was behind me sitting at the kitchen table cutting okra into little pieces. The knife made a clicking noise. I watched the old man, my grandpa, Oscar James Robinson. He wore overalls and his face was pink. He didn't talk much. His hair was white. He leaned over a can on the floor beside him. Brown tobacco juice fell from his lips and I heard it splat in the can.

My father was sitting in a chair. David, my brother, was standing between his legs. Daddy was smoking a cigarette. He was quiet. I wanted to run over to where my Daddy was and be safe there with David. It was a long, long way to go. It would be 50 years before I fully understood just how far it was. It's been a long road to a place in my father's arms, standing beside my brother.

I looked at Mama and she smiled and said, "Whatcha doin', hon?"

I said, "Nuthin'."

Then the old man squirted a brown stream of spit and it hit the hot stove. When the tobacco juice hit the stove it made a fizzy sound and a little puff of smoke appeared and whirled into the air. I laughed and looked at Daddy and David and wanted to run over and get between Daddy's legs with David.

Grandpa did it again and the sound was loud when he went "spitooie." There was the sound of sizzling tobacco juice and a little curl of smoke went up into the air. I laughed and looked at Daddy and David. David grinned and looked up at Daddy.

Grandma Lizzie yelled from the kitchen, "Oscar, don't do that in front of the children."

He looked right at me and smiled. I looked at him. Then he winked at me and growled, "Come over here." Oscar had survived a rugged life on his little Arkansas farm. He had raised four boys, Athen, Alton, Clem and my daddy. Oscar looked at me and with a motion of his hand beckoned me to come toward him. I stared at him.

There was something about him that frightened me. The look on his face was sad and angry at the same time. He growled at my father, "Just one flower when I go, Grade." My father was silent. My grandpa spit again onto the hot stove. Fssst! "Just one flower's all I'll be needin'. We dipped them steers, didn't we, Grade? Ever' damn one of 'em."

"Oscar! Watch your language!" Grandma Lizzie yelled from the kitchen door.

"They wasn't no ticks on them cows."

Daddy shook his head quietly in agreement.

"We dipped 'em, Pap," he said.

I ran to Mama and leaned on her leg and laid my head down in her lap. My mother was soft and smelled good. I was safe and happy. Later I walked back to the doorway and peaked around the corner.

"Let's eat, Oscar," Grandma Lizzie said.

They walked into the kitchen. I watched the old man but stayed close to Mama. We ate Sunday dinner. I begged for the pullie-bone of the fried chicken that just hours earlier walked in the back yard with the other chickens. This was the one they caught. Daddy took the head of the chicken in his hand and twirled the chicken around and around like Will Rogers doing a lariat rope trick until the head popped off. The chicken continued to flop around on the ground without a head. The head was in Daddy's blood-stained hand. Then when I looked more closely at his Sunday white shirt, tiny red dots of blood looked like Christmas lights.

I liked the mashed potatoes; they were smooth and without lumps. The best were the biscuits when you pulled them apart and put butter and jelly on them. I liked milk at home, but there was something wrong with the milk in the jug on the table. Yellow things were floating around on the top of the milk. I sat by Mama and she fixed me a biscuit. I picked it up and bit into it and felt the warm soft biscuit inside my mouth with the cool jelly on top of the melted butter.

"Is that good?" Mama asked.

"Yes," I said.

After we ate, Grandpa said, "Well, let's go t' the barn, boys." All the men must go to the barn to see the horse and feed the pigs.

Daddy, David and Grandpa walked toward the front door. I looked at Mama. She looked at Daddy. As they put on their coats, Mama said, "Grady." He turned to look at her and she pointed to me. He looked surprised. "Oh, you want to go with us, bud?" Daddy asked.

I ran to the front door. Mama brought my coat and I put it on by myself. Mama bent down to button my coat. Her black hair fell over her face and she pulled it back with one hand as she kissed my cheek.

We walked toward a big gate, opened it, then walked into a muddy barnyard where chickens walked around pecking at the ground. I didn't like chickens and stayed close to Daddy. He tossed his cigarette to the ground and a chicken looked at it. Daddy had very big hands. They were brown and big and I held on to one finger.

We walked into the barn and Grandpa looked up and pointed at something. Way up high I saw bunches of things hanging from the ceiling and the walls. Grandpa said, "Tobacco, onions, corn. Lotsa tobacco this year. I'll give you some, Grade."

A big pile of potatoes was stacked in the corner with white stuff sprinkled on them. It was hard to breathe in the barn. The air was smelly.

There was a big horse in a stall. It was brown and had white spots on the legs. I wanted to touch the horse. I walked over to the stall and tried to reach through the boards.

"James! Get back from there," Daddy yelled. It scared me and I jumped back and ran to where he was standing.

"Stay away from that horse, bud."

Grandpa opened the door and went into a dark room. He came out carrying a big bucket. He walked outside and then back in with the bucket full of water. He set it down and went back into the room. He came back out with a sack in his arms and poured white powder into the bucket. Daddy stirred it with a big stick as Grandpa poured the powder in and mixed it with the water. It looked like cold gravy with brown things floating around in it.

"Daddy, let me stir it," I said.

"No, James, get back."

Then Daddy picked up the bucket and we all walked out back of the barn. Daddy held his other arm way out and the stuff in the bucket spilled over on his Sunday pants.

"Careful, Grade," Grandpa said. "Here, let me get it."

"Nah, I got it, Pap," Daddy said.

We followed him to a pen, and then I saw and heard hogs. I ran toward the fence and David started running and passed me. He could run faster because he was older and bigger. We looked through the fence at the big hogs with hair on their backs. They snorted and grunted. Little pigs ran around and squealed. We laughed at them. The air was filled with a bad smell. I held my nose. "They stink," David said, and we laughed.

"Pe-e-e-e-u-u-u-u!" David said. I laughed again. I said, "Pe-e-e-e-u-u-u-u."

Daddy lifted up the big bucket and poured it over the fence. The hogs snorted and grunted, the pigs squealed and they stepped all over each other and into the trough.

Then David said, "Let me help, let me help."

"OK," Daddy said. "Put your hand on the bottom of the bucket and push up."

"Let me help, too," I yelled and ran to help.

"Get back, James. You'll get this stuff all over you."

David was older and bigger and he could do many more things than I could. I couldn't wait until I was as big and smart as David. Then maybe Daddy would let me do things, too.

I ran to the house and into the kitchen where Mama and Grandma Lizzie laughed and told stories. Grandma Lizzie was always laughing and talking, and Mama laughed with her in the warm kitchen. I watched from the kitchen door as the men folk fed the hogs. David carried the empty bucket toward the barn.

"Wilma, I don't think he'll ever get over it," Lizzie said. "Grady and Oscar dug that dipping vat out there with pick and shovel. Lordy, it was hot."

"He told me," Mama said. She walked to one door and stood beside me.

"They drug 200 head o' cattle through that vat. Dipped 'em all, shipped 'em on the train. Slept with 'em to Kansas City."

"I know, Lizzie."

Lizzie seemed quiet. "Found a tick on one cow," she sighed and wiped her face with the dish towel. "They quarantined the whole herd. I don't think Oscar ever got over it, Wilma," Lizzie said, staring out the window.

"Maybe not," Mama sighed and pulled me close.

"Grady loaned us the money to get the farm back. That's why Oscar says he wants only one flower on his grave."

I looked at Mama. She smiled at me.

A Short Bus Ride

I waited for Daddy's bus to come over the hill. I sat on my big rock at the end of the driveway and waited. Almost every day after school Daddy stopped the bus in front of our house and I rode with him to the bus shed. I loved being with my daddy. I looked back up the hill where his school bus would soon appear returning from his after school bus route. I listened for the sound of the engine. I held my breath and listened for the low rumble of the engine and hum of the tires that could be heard from over the hill before the bus appeared. There was no sound.

I turned to look back down Main Street. Far down the sidewalk I saw my brother David. He looked like a tiny little speck as he walked the one mile from his first grade classroom. He walked all by himself all the way home carrying his new Roy Rogers lunch bucket and a book. I couldn't wait until I got as old and as big and as smart as David and would walk to school and get a new lunch bucket and my own Big Chief tablet and a big thick pencil. He was smart.

At night he sat on the living room floor and did his homework and was constantly yelling into the kitchen where Mama cooked supper. He asked her very hard questions about numbers and letters. One day he said, "Mama, what is four and three?" She yelled back into the living room, "Four and three is seven." I watched as David carefully wrote down some numbers. "Mama," he asked again, "what is seven and three?" She said, "Seven and three is ten." Once again he wrote it down. Next year I would be just like David.

So I yelled into the kitchen, "Mama, what's four?" I waited for her to change the number and yell back to me. She said, "Four is just four!" They laughed. I looked at David. What's so funny? Sometimes when I said things everyone laughed and I didn't know why. So I tried again, "Mama, what's seven?" Seven was the same number that David had just used and she had turned into ten. Seven had to be ten because she just said it was and David wrote it down on his tablet.

"James, seven is just seven." I laughed very hard at my joke before they did but I wasn't sure what was funny. This time it was not as funny to the others. So I was the only one laughing. Maybe it was just the "4" that's funny and the "7" is not as funny. I didn't know.

David could write, too. As he learned the letters of the alphabet in school he practiced them by writing them on an imaginary blackboard, in the air. He walked around the house writing in the air with his finger. I watched him but I couldn't figure out the letters. He walked through the kitchen, stopped and then began writing in the air with his finger. Even at the table or at the grocery store or driving in the car his finger was always moving in the air. At the dinner table one night he wrote a word, looked at it for a long time and then said, "Mama, how do you spell 'fence'?"

She said, "Don't do that at the dinner table. But fence is spelled..." then she spelled fence.

I walked through the living room with my finger in the air making circles, and I said, "Mama, how do you spell?"

"How do you spell what, hon?" She looked at me funny.

I said, "How do you spell like, a word!"

"Oh," she said. "You have to pick out a word." I didn't know how to do that. I'd have to go to school to learn school work.

I wanted my daddy to come over that hill and stop for me. From my rock, I watched as David approached. He was near the Heard house and would soon be near the Fields' house where Eugene lived. After one more hold-your-breath pause listening for the low hum of the school bus, I ran toward the sidewalk. He walked very slowly and slightly wobbly with his right hand waving in the air like he was leading a band. I stopped at Monroe Street and looked both ways and then crossed to the sidewalk. I asked many questions, "Hi, whatcha' doin'? Where ya' goin? Whatcha' writin'? Gonna' ride the bus with Daddy today? Huh? Huh?"

He was very tired from the long day in the first grade, the walk home, and all that writing, and didn't appear to be too interested in my questions. He walked in the front door still waving his finger and disappeared.

I ran back to the rock and waited. The rock was round and made a perfect Fort. It was a Rocket Ship, Bus, Boat, Batter's Box, Basketball Court, Ball Field, and everything else that I would ever need. The bus would roar over the hill and sometimes, but not always, slow down and then stop. The door would open and there was Daddy smoking his cigarette, wearing his coaching cap and with his whistle around his neck attached to a tennis shoelace. He'll let me wear the whistle and blow it.

"Huh-oh. Listen, listen! An engine! A big engine. That's it!" I heard the low rumble. The school bus was approaching the horizon of the hill, louder. I heard the rumble of the school bus on the dirt road. Just before it appeared at the top of the hill the sound would change because the dirt road suddenly became smooth pavement.

Yes, it was the bus coming my way. I waved. The horn honked. He saw me. I hoped he would slow down and stop. From the top of the hill to my rock was not very far. It seemed like a long wait, listening for the engine to slow down. The tires were slowing down. He was stopping for me!!

The yellow bus with black front fenders stopped beside my rock. The door opened, and there he sat puffing the cigarette, blue baseball cap, and the whistle around his neck.

"Hi, Daddy!"

"Whaddya say, buddy-boy?"

"Hi, Daddy!" I climbed the steps of the bus, crawled behind his seat and plopped down on the heater next to him. Mama appeared at the front door of the house.

"We'll work the garden a little bit," he yelled to her.

"OK! See if any okra or green beans are ready," she yelled back.

"Where's David?"

"He's too tired to go work the garden, Daddy," I said quickly.

"He's eating his snack!" Mama yelled back.

"OK," he waved and I waved too. The bus began to roll down the hill toward the school and the bus shed.

"Whatcha' doin', Daddy? Where we going? Let's go downtown and around the square one time, please?"

"Can't do it, Hoss. School rules."

"Oh. You gotta game tonight?"

"Nope. Basketball season is over."

The ride was short. We drove down the hill, past the McLendon home, turned left into the high school, through the gates to the football field, and into the wooden bus shed.

We parked the bus and got out. We walked toward the garden. At the rock gym I said, "Let's race."

I always asked Daddy to race me so I could show him how fast I was and that someday I will be the fastest halfback on his team and he will stare out to the field when he's coaching on the sidelines and he will see me.

"Hey, Daddy, let's race to the end of the sidewalk."

"Not today, Hoss. I'm too tired."

"Come on, Daddy, just to the end."

I took off running and turned around to see if he would race me. He started to run. I turned on the speed and ran as fast as I could. I heard his keys and pocket knife and change and cigarette lighter jangle together in his pocket, and I knew where he was by the noise. He was right behind me but he couldn't catch me. I was too fast. I saw his long legs beside me out of the corner of my eye as I ran very fast.

"The end! I won."

"Yep, you're too fast for me."

I ran as fast as I could and I stayed just ahead of him. I was really fast. Someday I would run up and down the football field for him. And he would see me.

The Canary Reader

Mrs. Bell said, "James, your turn to read." I looked down at the book in my lap. There was a picture of a dog jumping over a fence. His name was Spot. A boy named Dick stood nearby and a girl named Jane was in the picture. Dick was talking to Jane, telling her to look at Spot and watch him jump over the fence. I looked at the words. I knew the words. "'Look, Jane, see Spot jump,' said Dick." I knew the words but I couldn't say them out loud in front of the other kids who sat in the circle with me.

"James, go ahead. Your turn to read," Mrs. Bell said again.

My head seemed to weigh a million pounds as I looked down at the words on the pages of the book. My mouth would not move. It could move and say those words but something deeper, bigger, wider, unknown, life-shaping would not allow me to move my mouth and say any words.

"James, we can't wait all day."

David read this very book last year. He sat at the kitchen table and read the whole thing out loud to Mama, and I watched and listened. He had been the best reader in his whole class. David had been put in the Redbird reading group along with two other good readers. In just a few days we would be divided into different reading groups: The Redbirds, Bluebirds and Robins. The smart kids, the average kids and the rest of us.

"Try again, James. 'Look, look' who?" Mrs. Bell paused and waited. I didn't look up but some of the other kids were giggling and squirming. I hated when kids laughed *at* me.

"Look, look, Jane..." I said.

"Good, keep going now."

I had decided *not* to read and prove to all of them that I was not as good a reader as David. I kept my head down and stared at the words on the paper and the bright yellow hair of Dick and Jane. It would be better not to try than to get a lot of words wrong in front of the teacher and the other kids. Then they would know for sure that I couldn't read as well as David.

"OK, next. Sharon, your turn. James, you stay in at recess."

That night, the phone rang at our house.

"Hello," I said.

"Is Wilma there?"

"Yes."

"May I speak to her?"

I recognized the voice. It was Mrs. Bell, my teacher.

"OK."

Mama dried her hands on a dish towel as she walked to the phone. I ran into her bedroom and crawled into the closet and shut the door. It was dark in the closet and I smelled the smoke in Daddy's clothes. I could hear her voice on the phone talking to my teacher.

"Uh-huh."

"Yes. Uh-huh."

"Well, he really likes to look at the books here at home."

"Maybe so."

"That might work. Yes, put him in a special group."

"Uh-huh. Well, thanks for calling. I'll see what I can do here. OK, thanks, Mrs. Bell."

Footsteps echoed through the thin walls as she walked back into the kitchen to finish the dishes. It was quiet in the closet. Quiet and dark and safe.

I stayed in the closet for a long time, moments, hours, months, years and eons so they would not know.

Meanwhile, back in the world of measurement, standards, division and valuing, stringent and rigid rules it was time for judgment day, the reading groups. Group evaluation in the second grade would determine life's destiny future success. On the way to school that day, David gave me instructions. Everyone in town knew it was Group Day. If your child made Redbirds, the party line would be alive with congratulatory messages for the proud parents. Announcements would be made at the Ladies Bible Class at the First Baptist Church. At the Conoco station, Bub Richards would say to customers as he pumped gas, "I wonder what reading group James got in?" Bud Corbin would stop embalming the dead for a day, or perhaps the dead would arise and ask, "What group did he get in?"

"James," David said as we trudged up the hill we called Grade School Hill, "they are going to do the reading groups today."

"I know, I know."

"So what group will you be?"

"I don't know. Mama says it don't matter."

"Well, just don't be in the Canary group. That's the worst one. They put the dumb kids in there and sometimes they don't ever get out."

"Get out of where?"

"That group."

"Ever?"

"Never, ever in all eternity. Once you get in that Canary reading group you'll be in it the rest of your life!"

"Oh, hell!"

"What did you say?"

"Nothing."

When I arrived at school all the talk was about the reading groups.

"Jack Lester, what group do you think you'll be in?" I asked my long-time church friend.

"I don't know!" Lester screamed in agony. "I woke up early and I can't stand not knowing."

The chairs were placed in circles. Books sat on each chair. Brand new books were placed in the chairs of the Redbird and Bluebird circles. In the Robins' circle was a used book with Dick and Jane stories. There were only three circles of chairs. Good, I thought to myself, only three groups.

"OK, kids, listen for your name to be called. The first group I call will come to the circle of chairs and you will be Redbirds. Everyone stand and come to the front of the room." We all stood and hurried to the front of the room and lined up in front of the chalkboard.

"When I call your name, go to the proper circle of chairs. The Redbirds will be..." and she called out the names of very smart kids, mostly girls, and Tim Woody. How did a boy get in the smart group? As their names were called they walked to the circle, picked up the new readers and sat down.

"Now, the next group we will call Bluebirds." As she called their names, each walked to their chairs and picked up their books and sat down. I looked at Mrs. Bell. She was checking her list. Please, please call my name. I held my breath and hoped she would call one more, James Robinson.

"Now the Robins." Shoot, I knew I'd be a Robin. She called out the list of names and they walked to the circle of chairs and picked up the battered, coverless books left over from the first grade.

I stood alone at the chalk board. All the Redbirds, Bluebirds and Robins busily flipped through the pages of their readers. Must be a mistake, I thought, as a lump formed in my throat and I tried to decide if I should sit down, or if I should attempt to move. Neal Wade looked up and saw me at the chalk board. He whispered something to the Robins. They giggled and looked at me. I raised my hand.

"Mrs. Bell," I said out loud, "did you forget me?"

She laughed and many of the kids laughed, too. I couldn't figure out why people laughed at me. Everyone looked at me standing there alone. Deep shame burned into my heart with each passing second. They were laughing at me again.

"No, James, I didn't forget you."

"So, am I in a group or anything?"

Everyone stared. My face felt very hot. I stood on one foot and held onto the eraser tray. White chalk dust covered my hands. The dusty smell of chalk filled my nostrils.

"James, I didn't forget you. You're in a special group."

A special group? Set apart from the other kids. I'm different from the other kids. I can feel it. I know I am. I've always known that I'm different.

"You're in the Canary group," she said with a smile. "I'll meet with you at recess."

The Canary group didn't have a circle. I was the only one in it.

Fishhook

"James," Daddy barked, "better find your ball glove, Hoss. You're gonna' be in right field tomorrow."

It had finally happened. I would be playing in my first real baseball game on a real field in the exciting Pee Wee League Tournament. It was impossible to sleep that night thinking about playing in a real game with David and the other boys.

During the long drive to Fort Smith I sat in the back seat and pounded my fist into my Stan Musial glove and listened to the gang talk and laugh. And then, yes, that word again, something about a fishhook. Why a fishhook at a baseball game? From what I could gather from the talk of the older and much more worldly boys, a fishhook scare happened at the plate when you batted. I had never batted in a real game before so there was much to learn.

As we piled out of the car and ran for the field I told Daddy that I would not be going to the plate to bat. "I'll play outfield, Daddy, but I don't want to bat."

He glanced at me and said, "You'll do fine, Hoss. Get up there and take your cuts. Be a little man."

Joe Stafford had a cousin in Barling whose name was Tommy Smith. His older brother was Hal Smith, the actual catcher for the St. Louis Cardinals where Stan The Man played. It was hard to imagine that a kid from our area had a brother who played major league baseball but it was true. Hal Smith's little brother was also a great baseball player and they called him Fishhook.

So, that was it. What an odd nickname, I thought. To name a guy after fishing equipment probably meant that he really liked to fish like my Daddy and fished so much that his friends started calling him Fishhook.

"Fishhook?" I laughed and said, "What a funny name!"

I sat on the bench in the real dugout and pounded my fist in the Stan Musial glove and thought about catching high fly balls and the chocolate malt that I would get at Zestos after the game.

"There he is," Joe said and pointed across the diamond. David and some of the other older boys looked at the other bench. I looked too and saw for the first time Tommy Fishhook Smith. He wore a baseball uniform with a red-sleeved shirt and red baseball cap. He wore red socks and black baseball spikes. He was very, very big and had a dark complexion. His jaw bulged with a chaw of tobacco and he spit on the ground and adjusted the protective cup in his pants. The bulge of the cup was the size of a hubcap.

The game was about to begin. Fishhook walked to the mound and threw a warm-up pitch. It streaked to the plate in a blur and slammed the catcher's mitt. Thwapp!! David and Joe looked at each other and their eyes got big and even Dave said, "Wow!"

I walked over to Daddy and said, "Daddy I'll play outfield but I don't want to bat."

He was smoking his cigarette and looked out to the mound where Fishhook warmed up.

"Jamesey, if you're big enough to play outfield you're big enough to bat. Just remember. He puts his pants on just like you do, one leg at a time."

I looked out to the mound at Fishhook's pants. He spit tobacco juice. He had hair on his thick brown arms and needed a shave.

The first pitch rocketed to the plate and slammed into the mitt. "Strike!" the umpire said.

Daddy was coaching at third base. "Take a cut boys, you can hit him. Time it right! Here we go!"

Three batters walked to the plate and faced three pitches and walked back to the dugout.

"Wow, you oughta see that hook!"

"What hook?" I said.

"Fishhook's hook!"

Oh, so that's why they call him Fishhook. A hook pitch. But what could that be?

I ran to right field as fast as I could run and stood in my place. When I arrived at my spot I turned and looked for Mama and waved. Each time I waved, she waved back and laughed.

David threw the ball to the plate and they hit it. The ball came out to me once and I ran to the fence and picked it up and threw toward where people were running and screaming. Finally everybody started running back to our dugout so I went too.

We ran back out to the outfield where I waved at Mama and she laughed and waved back so I waved again and she waved again and then I heard the voice of my father from the dugout like it was right on top of me "James!! Watch the ball! Play ball out there!"

One time a ball came my way and I threw down my Stan Musial glove and started running after it. I could really run fast when I put my head down. The ball bounced and bounced and I almost had it but it bounced again and then it hit the fence and I picked it up and gave it to somebody.

When we ran in to our dugout for the third inning there was His voice again growling, "Terry's up, Woody on deck and little Rob'son in the hole. Get a bat and loosen up." He called me by my last name. My own father. Why? I did not plan to bat but there was some misunderstanding about the situation. Apparently Daddy and the rest of the team thought I would go up to face Fishhook.

The first batter was up in the third inning and it seemed like a perfectly good time for me to go to the bathroom. I walked down the third base side of the field and past the outfield fence and entered the cinder block outhouse. I opened the stall door and closed it and locked it behind me. I looked down at the wooden toilet and held my breath against the stinky smells of the outdoor toilet in mid summer. There I remained, silent, alone, safe. Rather than go up and face the monster, I would stay locked inside. I was the only one who could unlock that door. I was the least important player on the whole team. No one would even notice. I stood there and pretended in the smell I was at home riding my bike down the hill feeling the cool breeze on my face.

"James!" the deep gravelly voice of Zeus thundered through my dreams, "Get out of there, you're up to bat!"

"I don't want to."

"James, come out of there right now."

I unlocked the stall door and walked out into the sun where Daddy stood holding a bat. He stuck the bat in my hand and said, "Hoss, you have to go up to bat if you're gonna be in the game." We hurried up the path toward home plate. Everyone looked at me and waited as I walked toward the batter's box, alone, holding a bat.

Then I heard his voice again, this time in a different tone, a tone that I heard on rare occasions from him, a voice of tenderness and love, a tone that I longed for. "James!"

I turned around.

He was walking toward me. "You scared, son?"

"What does that hook thing do?"

He hunkered down on one knee. He put his arm around my shoulders and I could smell the familiar aroma of tobacco and his sweat-stained ball cap.

"Time out ump. He's a little nervous. I'll coach him."
We stood at home plate. "Now hold your bat just like this. And old Fishhook is going to throw that ball. He throws a pretty good curve ball. Now, he'll throw it up here and it'll be coming right at your head."

"It will?"

"Yeah, he'll throw it right up here. But don't you duck!"

"Don't duck?"

"No sir. See, that's what that hook is. He's got a dang good curve ball for a young fella. It'll look like it's gonna hit you but then it'll break right down over the plate. So you have to hang in there and wait for it to break. "

"Oh."

"All right now get up there and get set. And don't you duck."

Everyone was looking at me. "You can do it, James! Swing that bat!"

"Pull the trigger now, little Robinson."

"Hang in there and take your cuts!"

"Be a little man, now, and swing that bat."

Just don't duck.

Be a man.

Fishhook wound up and fired the ball. I stood there in my tennis shoes and my blue baseball cap and watched the white blur approach the plate and heard it buzz through the air getting nearer and nearer much quicker than I had thought possible. Daddy was right. It was coming right at my head. But I had the secret message: Don't duck. The ball was spinning right beside my blue baseball cap and I waited for it to curve downward over the plate for the strike and maybe I would swing and hit the ball. The faint smell of horsehide mingled with the hum of spinning threads inches from my head and I waited for the ball to do what my Daddy said it would do.

Suddenly little stars appeared all over the ball field, sparkly lights of red, green, blue, lots of blues flashed off and on and swirled together around my head. The air seemed to vanish from my lungs, leaving me without air to breath. Loud bells rang in my head. The umpire in a thick metal mask looked down at me from upside down. I heard him say. "You OK?"

Something has gone wrong here.

My father looked down into my face.

"James, you OK, Hoss?"

"Uh-huh! Yeah, I'm OK."

"Atta boy! Get up now. Go to first!"

I got up. My head was pounding. The colors and outline of objects like dugouts, trees, fences and people seemed blurring and running together.

"Don't cry. Go to first."

I looked for Mama in the stands and walked a few steps toward the backstop where she was sitting. Then I saw her standing against the fence looking at me sadly. "You OK, hon?"

"James!" the voice said, "first is over yonder. Hurry."

I must go to first base. But I am dizzy and can't seem to focus on a direction.

A Once-In-A-Lifetime Dive

I peered down through the willow leaves into the white and green water of Jackass Junction, concentrating, psyching myself, gaining courage to execute a dive that no other sane human would dare attempt. This performance, I was convinced, would live forever in the minds of those who watched. I would win the prize. I would be the hero.

My toes ached from gripping the willow branches between them. My lily-white, bare bottom flashed brazenly through the trees at passing motorists on Highway 10, only a few yards away.

"Do it!" they screamed from below.

"I'm goin', I'm goin'," I said. I had to. It was too late to back out. You didn't climb down the willow tree.

Most of the guys had already performed their top vote-getting dives. Each in turn had climbed the tree, verbally described to all present their own personal dive — and jumped. But this would be my all time best, the once in a lifetime: a forward-flip-catch-a-Snickers-in-midair (thrown from the creek bank at the precise moment)-and-eat-it-before-you-hit-the-water dive. A feat to shame all other attempts, the World Series of belly whoppers.

It all started in May of 1957, these daily treks to the best swimming hole around Greenwood. We rode old fenderless bicycles out to the second bridge on Highway 10. Usually the whole gang showed up, and just about everybody rode a bicycle. Everybody, that is, except Wayland T. Jackson. He never rode a bicycle. He usually just appeared out of the bushes, or someone would spot him wading from upstream or crawling through the thick brush along the banks. We'd be swimming or playing chase when all of a sudden there would be Wayland T. with that strange look on his face. His family had moved into town from a far-off region — Louisiana or somewhere. He never said much and never joined in the races or the diving contests. He was very skinny and had olive-green skin and slanted brown eyes. Everyone thought Wayland T. was a little strange. One day he brought a snake to school. That did it; everyone knew then that Wayland T. had not been blessed with a full deck. Any sane, normal, red-blooded American was deathly afraid of snakes, especially cottonmouth water moccasins.

During the summer, the intrusion of a cottonmouth was the only thing that could separate us from the cool waters of Jackass Junction. An Arkansas thunderstorm couldn't budge us, even the kind that rolled in from southwest Oklahoma, spewing lightning bolts like buckshot. Nor could a tornado approaching from over Backbone Mountain or the blessed news of an unprotected watermelon patch. Only one thing, one obscene word — snake — could empty the water in an instant.

But now I was ready to dive. "OK," I yelled at Billy Joe, my designated Snickers thrower, "don't throw until after I come out of the flip, you hear? After!"

"Yeah, got it," he replied. "You ready?"

"No, for God's sake, no," I whispered, but they couldn't hear me.

David, my older brother, who was better than me at everything, had performed his famous cherry-bomb dive, a real crowd pleaser. He jumped from the tree, whistling through his teeth on the way down, then he grabbed his knee and hugged it up to his chest just before he hit the water. Twweeeee *ker-BOOM!* Water shot high into the air. It was majestic and impressive.

My main competition, however, was from my old friend and companion, Joe Stafford, a diminutive, but extremely fast, second baseman on the Little League team. Joe's dive was called the cow-pasture-sprint-leap-over-the-barbed-wire-fence-head-first-special. Truly a magnificent expression of adolescent creativity, coupled with raw nerve and just a dash of sheer idiocy. The kid was fast. He backed off out through the pasture of the Circle L Ranch and, after a deep breath, began the sprint. Dodging rocks, stickers, stumps and fresh cow piles, he approached the fence and dived through the barbed wire with reckless abandon. A very gutsy move for a skinny-dipper. He then crashed through the thick bushes at the water's edge and tumbled into the water.

I knew that it would be almost impossible to top that number. In order to win the diving prize, a sack of Hershey bars, a Jitterbug fishing lure and two melted Snickers, I'd have to come up with a real showstopper. I had been standing there almost 20 minutes. The sun was setting and the white-faced Herefords were moving slowly toward the pasture gate.

"OK, this is it," I yelled again. "You ready, Billy Joe? You ready to throw?"

"Ready!"

"You sure?"

"Yeah, I'm sure," he screamed. "Now go, will ya?"

"Here goes."

I looked once again at the water. It was like concrete if you landed just wrong. I jumped, and my world turned upside down.

I began the never-before-attempted forward-flip-catch-Snickers-in-midair-and-eat-it-before-you-hit-the-water dive. It was my moment in time. In all of Sebastian County and the universe, I was on center stage. I forced my head forward, anticipating the proper momentum. I knew I'd have to get the flip over with as quickly as possible so as to concentrate on the Snickers that would come at me like a chocolate fastball.

From my upside-down position, I saw a hawk make a right (or was it a left?) turn. Like a clicking camera shutter, I saw scenes pass before my eyes, focused for only a split second before disappearing. Herefords upside down toward their afternoon feeding, dirt bank, willow tree trunk, willow tree top, blue sky, opposite bank, staring faces, green foamy water.

Then — just as Billy Joe drew his arm back to throw the Snickers — someone screamed, "Snaaaaake!"

The word sent chills through my gyrating body.

"Snake! Snake! Snake!" they screamed in panic. I lost what little control I had and came out of my forward flip somewhere south of China, flipping, twisting, legs pumping like pistons. I saw a chocolate brown blur coming at me against a background of scampering bodies, leaves and spraying water.

Where was the snake?

I reached out frantically in the general direction of the blur and felt a stinging sensation on the right side of my face as the candy bar hit with surprising impact. I grabbed it and shoved in into my mouth as my tender stomach hit the surface of Jackass Junction.

Where is the snake? What kind is it? Is it true they can't bite underwater? Screams of panic echoed across the pastureland.

"Look, it's a granddaddy! Lookit the size of that thang!"

I was underwater with a mouthful of Snickers and muddy creek water. I couldn't breathe, but that was not half as important as the location of the intruder. The Devil King swam somewhere in the same pool with the naked I.

They were still ranting about the size of the cottonmouth when my head finally appeared above the surface.

"Get out, you idiot!"

I couldn't move because I was gagging for air. My front side was completely numb from the impact, and I was choking on the mixture of chocolate and muddy water. The snake was coming toward me. "Get out!" they screamed. I scrambled up the bank with goose bumps the size of golf balls.

"Lookit the size of that dude," Kenny said in awe. I looked for the first time and saw a huge cottonmouth water moccasin. With head triumphantly aloft, he slithered slowly and deliberately through the water only a few feet from the bank on which we were standing. Never again could I freely and without fear immerse myself in the cloudy green water of the Junction. The intruder, symbolic of another snake in another garden of innocence, paraded triumphantly the entire length of the pool and then returned as if to mock us one more time. We watched in helpless silence.

Then it happened. From the very top of the willow tree a trumpet call sounded forth across the fields.

"EEE-iiijjjhhhh." Plummeting through the air, descending straight down toward the huge cottonmouth, was none other than Wayland T. Jackson. "Snnnnnaaaaake diiiiiiive," he yelled. The once-performed, never-forgotten snake dive.

He hit the water directly on top of the snake and disappeared. The cottonmouth was nowhere to be seen and neither was Wayland T.

"Wayland T. is crazy!"

A dark spot appeared just beneath the surface of the water. It was the burr-head haircut of Wayland T. as he came up laughing and gasping for air.

"I got him," he said.

He raised his right arm from beneath the water. Leaves rattled as a dozen boys took one giant step backward, for the big cottonmouth was wrapped around Wayland T.'s skinny arm. His bony fingers couldn't reach around the snake as he crawled out on the dirt bank, being careful to hold the monster in expert fashion. The snake didn't appear disturbed; his tongue flicked and darted from his large head; his small eyes seemed to speak. Wayland T. smiled his funny little smile.

"He wins," someone said.

"Yeah, snake dive wins."

"Beautiful," said another.

A sack of melted Hershey bars, the Jitterbug lure and two Snickers landed at Wayland's feet. He picked up his faded Levi's with his left hand and tossed them over his shoulder and, with the cottonmouth curled round his arm and neck, sloshed upstream. He was licking melted chocolate from the Hershey wrapper and whispering to his new friend as he disappeared into the underbrush.

We dressed in uncommon silence.

"Did anybody see my dive?" I asked. "I caught the dang thing."

There was no answer.

Stan The Man Musial

As Mama gingerly placed a plate of fried chicken on the table, Johnny Antonelli laid a slow curve across the plate at Sportsmans Park in St. Louis. And as I reached out to grab the drumstick, Stan Musial uncoiled from his unusual corkscrew stance and lashed Antonelli's delivery over the rightfield pavilion for a home run. It was Sunday, May 2, 1954, and Harry (Holy Cow) Caray was broadcasting the first game of a doubleheader with the Giants over KWHN in Fort Smith, Ark. It was a day to remember — 25 seasons ago.

"Did you hear that? Stan the Man hit a home run!" I announced through a mouthful of chicken.

"Yeah," said Daddy, "and listen to ol' Harry now."

"Holy cow," we said, mimicking Harry in unison.

After our usual Sunday dinner of chicken, mashed potatoes and green beans, Daddy would lie in bed, puffing occasionally on a Prince Albert roll-your-own and listening to Caray in distant St. Louis describe the exploits of Stanley Frank Musial.

The Man was a legendary figure in our part of the country in 1954. He had already won the batting title six times and had been MVP three times. But such honors were not the only reasons that Stan was our Man. We kept in touch with the world through him. Musial was, I felt, my personal representative in faraway, mysterious regions like Philadelphia, Chicago, and that ultimate, unfathomable place, New York.

I had never seen a major league ballplayer and didn't consider that fact unusual. Those other places, those other people, those other kids had the boys of summer. They had Hodges. They had Snider. They had Mantle and the Empire State Building. Bostonians had Ted Williams and Paul Revere and the entire Revolutionary War. And what did kids in Arkansas have? Revivals. The county fair. The Ozarks. And, by adoption, Stan the Man, our only person, institution, phenomenon or product that was superior to what they had. The Man was ours, mine, and he was the greatest.

It rained very hard early that day, and there wasn't any batting practice. I never felt too good about playing a game without looking at a few balls in the strike zone, so, naturally, I was a little uneasy about hitting that day. Antonelli was a very good fastball pitcher and had a good curve to go with it. I was just trying to meet the ball, figuring I'd be a little unsure. He came in with a curve and I tried to swing level. I always hit off the fastball — I mean, I was set up for the fastball, then I could adjust to the slower speeds. I swung easy and level and happened to hit it good, and it went out. That was the first one of the day (Stan Musial).

By the fifth inning, Mama had the dishes washed and had put baby sister down for a nap. Then she tried to get a little sleep, too. My brother David was hitting rocks out of the driveway with a sawed-off broomstick. Daddy dozed in his undershirt, but kept one ear on the radio. I was on the front porch when the Man came up in the fifth.

The Giant pitchers never gave me the same pitch twice. Teams pitched differently to every player, and the Giants had the idea that I should never see the same pitch twice in a row. Antonelli was working me in that manner. Schoendienst was on, and Antonelli threw me a fastball, about the only one I saw all day. I took a good level swing at the ball and —

"Long fly ball to right...way back," screamed the voice over the radio. "It might be out of here." Daddy opened his eyes. David held the broom handle steady. "It is! A home run for Stan the Man Musial! Holy cow, his second of the day off Antonelli."

"Wow, Stan the Man hit another one!" I called to both of them from the front porch.

"Quit yelling into the window!" Mama pleaded.

Around 1:30 I was back in the kitchen looking for something to eat. I poured a bowl of Cheerios and milk and yelled to my father in the bedroom.

"What's the score?"

"Tied up 6-6"

"Who's pitching?"

"Kid named Hearn."

"When's Stan up?"

"Next."

"Quit yelling into the bedroom!" Mama said.

Jim Hearn came in for Antonelli, and it was tied at six-all. A couple of guys on base. I'd never hit three home runs in a game and didn't consider myself a home-run hitter, really. I was more of a line-drive type, but Hearn threw me a slider that got out over the plate, and so I took a good cut and —

"Way back!"

I sprang up from the table and ran from the kitchen through the living room to the open bedroom door.

"It might be out of here!" Daddy raised up on one elbow. "It could be...it is!"

Daddy laughed and said, "Holy cow!" as David and I jumped around the radio. Mama said, "Oh, for cryin' out loud," and got out of bed. "You don't mean he hit another one?"

For the second game of the doubleheader, Daddy moved the radio into the living room.

"You think he could hit another one, Daddy?" asked David.

"Sure he will," I volunteered. "Stan the Man is the greatest hitter of all time, isn't he, Daddy?"

"He might be, but we can't expect him to hit four in one day," said Daddy, whose opinion on hitting we highly respected because he had been a legendary batsman in Sebastian County. Rumor had it that around 1926 our dad hit four long ones over the pecan trees in Lucas, Arkansas, off a 15-year-old fireballer, pitching in overalls and bare feet, named Jay Dean. (He later was known as Dizzy Dean.) And down behind the courthouse, in 1945, Daddy had blasted a line drive off Warren Spahn, who was pitching for the Army team at Fort Chaffee. Yes sir, our daddy sure could hit a baseball.

The afternoon wore on. Musial walked in the first inning of the second game and flied out deep to Willie Mays his second time at bat. Not realizing the historical import of the day's events and being a restless kid, at about 5:30 I got on my bicycle and coasted to town. I happened to notice that Mr. Stafford was working overtime in the Greenwood Cleaners. As I walked toward the shop, he pulled down the press, causing steam to hiss loudly out of the side of the building. "Stan has hit three homers," I announced proudly as I entered. Mr. Stafford smiled and pointed to the radio, saying, "Yeah, I know, and he's up again next." He placed a pair of gray slacks on the bottom pad and brought the handle down while listening to the broadcast over the hissing.

Hoyt Wilhelm threw a knuckleball, and I didn't like to hit against that. By the time it got to the plate it was somewhere else from where you last saw it, if you know what I mean. It moved all over, and you just couldn't be sure where it was going to be. But on this particular occasion, I think he tried to slip a curve by me. I saw the ball spinning and —

"Way back!" Caray screamed for the fourth time, now with a kind of frenzy that tightened his voice box and caused a gagging sound. "It might be...it could be...it is!"

Mr. Stafford roared with laugher and held up four fingers of the hand that was not on the press. Steam and black smoke seeped out from between the pads of the press, and I wondered about those gray slacks. I squealed with delight and headed for the house as fast as I could pedal. Mama was getting ready to go to church, but us menfolk gathered around the radio to see if our Man could do it one more time. Daddy said the fourth homer had equaled a major league record for home runs in two successive games. The Man was the best.

After the fourth one, they told me in the dugout I had tied a record. I guess I was somewhat elated about that. Although I wasn't a home-run hitter, I naturally believed I could hit with most of them, so to hit four home runs in one day made me very happy. I guess my next at bat one of the few times in my whole career that I was thinking home run when I went to bat. I didn't swing for a homer, but I admit I was thinking about it even though I didn't feel I had a chance off the knuckleball. Wilhelm floated one up there, and I figured it looked about as good as any, so I swung and hit it well —

"Way back!" It was too much. David swung the broom handle like a maniac and fell backward over a footstool. I couldn't think of a thing to say that was loud enough, so I just jumped up and grinned and knew that the Man was my man. Even Mama got excited. She was on her way out the back door, with her Bible in one hand and little sister Jane in the other, when she heard the noise. She ran back to the living room door and watched us chant in unison, "Might be...it could be...IT IS! A home run! Holy cow! Stan Musial's fifth of the day!"

Daddy shook his head. With a faraway look on his face he said, "Well, I'll be damned." He wasn't supposed to say that on Sunday.

Mama said, "Grady, puh-lease!"

It was past 7:30 before Musial came to bat again in the ninth. I knew he would hit No. 6, but Daddy said we should be realistic. I figured, though, if he could hit five he could hit six.

They brought in Larry Jansen. I've never understood why they brought in the ace of their staff in the ninth to pitch to me. It was maybe the only time I ever swung for a home run. He threw a fastball that came in real good, and for some reason I took it. You know, I've always had a feeling that I should've hit that pitch. Then he threw me a fastball, high and in. I was too anxious and swung way too hard and popped the ball up to Whitey Lockman at first base.

David and Daddy ate cold chicken at the kitchen table. I stood in the middle of the living room and swung the broom handle, from the left side, crouched in that unique corkscrew stance of Musial. "The pitch [swoosh], long fly ball, way back, it might be, it could be, it is! A home run. Holy cow!"

The Day We Tackled
Bobby Joe Needham

Armageddon. That's the word I thought of when the football was snapped to 165-pound Bobby Joe Needham on the third night of junior high football practice, with me standing across the line in the defensive backfield trying desperately to look like a football player. Needham was a rock-hard 16-year-old who had flunked twice, was the son of a coal miner, smoked cigarettes, had fist fights with seniors and won, chewed tobacco and used four-letter words that most of us couldn't even spell. When he ran with the football he put both arms over it and stomped straight ahead.

So there I stood, all 94 pounds of savage seventh grader, frozen in time and space with spindly white legs spread valiantly over my turf on the 20-yard line.

I was wearing a football uniform. I was out for football. I preferred band, reading, the Mickey Mouse Club and wading in creeks, but my father was the head senior high football coach. I was out for football. I wore a black leather helmet, with no faceguard. It had a white leather top that from a distance looked exactly like an unburnt match. The helmet was more than 30 years old, right out of the Knute Rockne era. You could tell a seventh grade kid a mile away. That white top was like a beacon.

Everybody wanted to hit a seventh grader. The ninth graders loved to splatter seventh graders across the slick, dew-covered grass and then laugh. They had contests to see who could knock a seventh grader the farthest. Eighth graders always tried to hit a white-topper and naturally, fellow seventh graders looked for white-toppers because they were the only ones of equal size. Most seventh grade kids had one other dead giveaway — skinny legs. Skinny white legs were seventh grade. Legs with peach fuzz were eighth grade and muscular brown legs with hair were ninth grade. You dove headlong at skinny hairless legs. You were very careful not to hit legs with peach fuzz and a slight bulge of calf muscle. And legs with black curly hair and thick, hard calves like Bobby Joe Needham's you avoided like poison ivy.

The preacher said Armageddon would be the last battle before the end time. I figured without question this was my end time; I just hoped it would look like a battle.

Bobby Joe Needham burst through the line and I saw dust and dried brown grass fly up behind his steel cleats as he savagely ripped through two fellow white-topper linebackers. The first kid hit the left leg and the second crashed into his other leg at the same moment. They hit like bugs on the windshield of a heavy-duty Ford truck going down a long hill with a load of logs.

Needham grunted and snorted and made inhuman sounds. It was a very hot night, and I smelled like a man. Sweat dripped off my nose and the white-top helmet sat one-sided on my head with the elastic chinstrap dangling under my chin.

I wanted to run, but couldn't move a muscle. Just like the time we camped out in the mountains and I went looking for firewood and all of a sudden a strange man stepped out from behind a tree not two feet from my face and stared at me. I tried to scream and run that night, too, but all I could do was suck air and go, "that— tha— tha—."

I couldn't run. My Dad was the senior high coach and they were at the other end of the field. The senior high studs wore ducktails, pink shoes and matching socks, drove hot rod Fords with drag pipes and all of them could sing, "Peggy Sue, Peggy Sue, Prittie, Prittie, Prittie, Prittie Peggy Sue...."

I couldn't run. If I was going to be the next Lance Alworth, wear Razorback red, and play on Saturday in Fayetteville against the Baylor Bears, the Texas Tech Red Raiders, and the Texas Longhorns, I would have to stand my ground and become a Bulldog. So, goodbye, James Fenimore Cooper. Goodbye, *Cowboy Sam and the Rustlers*. Goodbye, Annette and..."

Hello, Bobby Joe Needham.

He was so close now, I could hear him snort. The images blurred before me. White-toppers were in hot pursuit. I smelled cigarette smoke and saw that mole under his left eye through his faceguard. His eyes were coal black because Bobby Joe Needham had been working the mines for two summers and this very day he had been two miles down in Number One at the Excelsior Coal Mine.

I hadn't moved a muscle since Needham got the ball. My feet were spread properly and firmly into the dusty, dirt-covered field. I wore rubber cleats, which also were for seventh graders. I guess they were afraid we would cleat ourselves or perhaps each other in the wild dog piles we called tackles.

Bobby Joe Needham lowered his rock-hard head. I saw thick neck muscles covered with brown, sweaty, leathery skin bulge just as the helmet slammed into my number 97 jersey. Bobby Joe grunted and snorted.

I saw the lights of the field. My white-topper popped off my head like a Roman candle going skyward and disappearing into the night, but the elastic chinstrap was squarely under my jaw and brought the Rawlings white-topper back to its original position with a thud. Lights came on all over the universe and bells jingled like Christmas and my entire life passed before me, all 12 wonderful years, and about two and a half I hadn't lived yet.

I heard Bobby Joe snorting, kids grunting as my body was being dragged down the field. I was on my back with my thumb somehow entangled in Bobby Joe's belt. Pumping furiously, his piston-like knees were a blur only an inch from my face. He couldn't run very fast with me banging against his legs, so seventh grade defenders were able to jump onto his back — three, four and five at a time, but that made him even more determined to go the length of the field.

My thumb hurt and I wondered if it would separate from my hand. I thought about my thumb and how it would look dangling from his belt. Then, it happened.

Bobby Joe, somewhat off balance due to the half dozen screaming seventh graders swinging from various parts of his anatomy, made a mistake. The steel cleat of his left shoe got caught in the elastic chinstrap of my leather helmet just long enough to cause him to stumble and come crashing, thrashing, raging to the dusty turf.

In a ghastly heap of moans and dust and sweat we lay. The dust cleared. One by one we peeled off. My face felt like a hot waffle. Out of one eye was nothing. Darkness.

"Atta boy, little Rob'son, way to hit, Hoss."

Bobby Joe got up slowly. I thought how ironic, the first tackle of my career and I lose an eye.

"I can't see," I screamed. "My eye, my eye, I can't see!"

Bobby Joe looked down at me.

I looked up at him through my remaining good eye.

"Nice tackle, little Rob'son," he smiled.

"I can't see," I insisted.

Bobby Joe reached out and slapped my leather helmet and it spun around on my head.

Suddenly I could see out of both eyes. "There ye go, Hoss, you were looking out the ear hole."

There is a magical moment in the life of every boy when he knows that he has earned his spurs. In my town, in my time, it was taking on the likes of Bobby Joe Needham.

I spit dirt and grass as I limped back to my position. I looked down the field to see if my father was watching.

Jazz Kittenz

The three bells calling school assembly sounded. Joe Stafford (coronet), Tim Woody (baritone), Bob Bailey (clarinet) and I (drums) hurried to our places behind the curtain as hundreds of kids eagerly fought for seats in the auditorium. Teachers, football players, cheerleaders, farm kids, town kids, greasers with slicked-back ducktails, majorettes and, of course, the Jazz Katz — all poured into the auditorium, happy to be out of class for just a little while, even to listen to four seventh graders attempt to play rock 'n roll.

Inspired by the success of Elvis, a group of talented senior musicians had formed a rock 'n roll band, the Jazz Katz. Before you could say "Rock Around The Clock," they had established themselves in Greenwood High School and throughout the greater Greenwood area. They played frequently in high school assemblies, an FHA convention at the Fort Smith Masonic Lodge, and a private birthday party for drum major Nancy Hocott.

It was 1957, and the whole world was falling apart. The Russians had a satellite called Sputnik orbiting the earth.

Nuclear holocaust was openly discussed in school. We prepared for a direct hit by crawling under our desks. I imagined a mushroom cloud on the school playground.

A direct nuclear hit was worrisome enough, but it was moral corruption the Baptists feared most. A book called *Peyton Place* shocked the nation. Adultery was openly discussed in the movie *The Seven Year Itch* starring Marilyn Monroe. That was bad enough, but it was the strangely pretty boy from Tupelo, Mississippi, with his gyrating pelvis that the Baptists viewed as the most obvious sign of moral corruption.

The drummer in the Jazz Katz was the Gene Krupa of Sebastian County, the Cozy Cole of 701 North Main...my brother, David. He was in the eighth grade.

The Jazz Katz were making a name for themselves and would soon hit the big time. Maybe that's why as I entered the bandroom one day for band practice, my seventh grade classmate Joe Stafford said, "James, you want to play the drums in the Jazz Kittenz?"

I couldn't imagine four seventh graders creating hot jazz, but Joe and Tim were two of the smartest boys in class. Bob was OK on the clarinet but was known for his occasional "Squeak" notes emitting from the instrument without warning. I didn't want to question their great idea. But me playing the drums?

"Sure," Tim said, "you can play drums."

"But I don't play the drums!"

"David does," Joe said.

Joe was right. Perfectly logical. David played the drums in the Jazz Katz as an eighth grader even though the rest of the group was made up of seniors. The logic was simple. David played drums, I'm David's brother, therefore, I could play the drums.

"All you have to do," Tim said, "is hit the snare drum on the down beat and the bass drum on the up beat."

"Which is which?" I asked.

"It doesn't matter. And you have to hit the cymbal every eighth note."

"How will I know an eighth note?"

"Never mind. Just so you keep time."

"What's 'time' mean?"

"You'll learn, don't worry."

We quickly set up the bass drum with the foot pedal and the snare drum on the drum stand and placed the cymbal beside it. Instant rock 'n roll drummer. Tim lifted the big baritone up to his lap and licked the mouth piece. Joe sat in his seat and jiggled the valves of his shiny coronet. Bob licked the reed of his clarinet.

We were set for our first practice. They looked at me. I waited for the wild rock 'n roll music to begin. And waited.

"James."

"Huh?"

"You start the song!"

"Me? How?"

"Like David does in the Jazz Katz," Tim said. "Yeah," Bob said excitedly, "it's really cool when he hits the rim of the drum 10 times and then Jimmie Didier and Davey Joyce stand up and start off. So you do that. Hit the rim 10 times."

I hit the side of the drum head, the rim, with the drum stick and counted each rap, "One-two-three-four...."

"Faster!" they all said.

"Huh?"

"You should hit the 10 licks at the same beat as the song "Rock Around The Clock." You know, like, tat-tat-tat-tat! Like the beat of the song."

"Oh, OK." I couldn't believe how much I was learning already about playing drums. It was so easy compared to the many notes of the coronet.

"Here we go, ready, one, two, three, four...," I yelled out, feeling much more confident now as I rapped solidly on the rim of the snare drum.

"Hold it!" Joe yelled.

"...five, six, seven...."

"Hold it, James!" Bob seemed a little upset and shook his head.

"What?"

"Don't actually say the number out loud as you hit it. Count to yourself and then on the tenth lick, we take over. OK?"

"OK. OK, let's try again."

We played "Rock Around The Clock" twice. One time we went all the way through without stopping, although on some parts it was only Tim tooting on the baritone horn and me thumping the bass drum

Word traveled like wild fire around school that day. A new group to challenge the mighty Jazz Katz would soon play for the whole school assembly. Sharon Pischier walked right up to me in the study hall one day and started talking to me. To me?!

"James, are you really in the Jazz Kittenz?" she asked with a kind of smile that I hadn't received from her since the second grade. She was stunningly cute. For one whole week in second grade Sharon had "liked" me.

"Yeah, I am. Drummer," I said nonchalantly.

"Just like Cozy?" she squealed, referring to David's nickname. "Cozy Cole."

"Oh, yeah," I said, trying to maintain my cool. "Just call me Cozy-Junior."

She laughed and ran back to the other girls.

Then one night, Tim called with great news. Our reputation had apparently spread throughout the school for we had been invited to make our debut in the next school assembly on Friday morning.

"Mama," David said during dinner, "you ought to hear them."

"I bet they are good," Mama said with eternal optimism and a big smile.

"They are awful! They only have three instruments and you just can't do rock 'n roll with a baritone horn, coronet and clarinet, even if you're Benny Goodman."

"Well, they'll do fine. Let's take our dishes over to the dish pan."

"James," David pleaded one last time, "you guys shouldn't try this. You need more practice. It won't go over very well."

On Thursday night I imagined my part while lying in bed. Thump the bass drum with the foot pedal on the down beat and bang down both sticks on the snare on the up beat, and every eighth beat or so reach out and give the cymbal a good lick. Tim and Joe said that cymbal part wasn't too important. That was a big break for me since I didn't know what an eighth note was. Stick to the basics, snare drum, bass drum. What could possibly go wrong?

On Friday morning I hurried to the band room. Joe arrived carrying his trumpet case. Bob and Tim wore their bow ties and white shirts and sported a surprise accessory: a colorful cap made famous by Ben Hogan, the golfer. They brought Joe and me a cap, too. I placed my cap on my head and looked in the mirror. I saw my freckled face, two big front teeth and the strange cap and a bow tie. Perfect. Rock and rolllll.

"Now, James," Joe began, "you've been losing count of the rim shots at the start. Keep the count right and don't stop after eight or nine and say, 'How many is that?'" We died laughing.

We sat behind the curtain in our snazzy outfits and listened to the low murmur of the entire school.

We heard Mr. Dill make an announcement and then say, "It's our custom here at GHS to encourage all of the students to participate in various extracurricular activities. So, here they are, the Jazz Kittenz!"

The curtains parted. I looked out into the smiling faces of the entire school. There was a brief moment of stunned silence. Then, a roar of laughter. A wall of sound hit me. Mouths were wide open as kids slapped their thighs and pounded the backs of the unfortunate person seated in front of them. I heard someone calling my name and looked toward the first rows where someone seemed to be screaming, "James! James!"

It was Joe, our trumpet player.

"Hit it!" he bellowed over the audience.

"Now?"

"Yes, now!"

I adjusted my seat and tapped the drum stick on the rim of the drum. But they couldn't hear it. So I started all over, this time with more force, but Joe and Tim didn't know I was starting over. So at the eighth lick, I stopped....

"How many is that?" I screamed. The roar of laughter from the audience increased.

"Keep on hitting it," Joe yelled and rolled his eyes. I banged away and at some point he stood all alone in his bow tie and Ben Hogan cap and as loudly as he could, blew the first notes of the famous Bill Haley and the Comets' song, "Rock Around The Clock."

Tah-dah, tah-dah, tah-dah, -dah, -dah. I hit everything I had with one lick, creating loud crashing sounds.

Then Tim scooted his chair back, stood up with his big baritone, licked his lips carefully and joined in the tune, repeating the first line only on a slightly higher note.

Tah-dah, tah-dah, tah-dah, -dah, -dah. I hit 'em again. Whump, clang, bang.

The crowd was into it now and attempted to clap along. The sound of our band was drowned out like a giant tidal wave roaring over a babbling brook.

Bob stood and joined in as I tried to hit the foot pedal and snare drum on alternate beats. And just as we feared, Bob, being somewhat inexperienced in the performing arts and understandably nervous, tightened his sensitive, highly trained lip just a smidge too tight, thus emitting, on his very first note, the mother of all squeak notes. Dogs ran for cover as far away as Oklahoma.

Mrs. Anna B. Adams, the senior English teacher and director of all senior class plays, was a very large woman with seemingly unmanageable gray hair. She was a brilliant teacher, everyone said, and would someday change the course of my life. Mrs. Ann trying to show support burst out with laughter, then clapped along and nodded her head on the beat, trying to help me with the mysterious element they called keeping "time." She held her hand against her ample bosom, apparently to ward off a heart malfunction. I could barely hear the boys in the band. From off stage, behind the curtain, I saw David. He was frantically motioning toward me in an animated way, apparently urging me to either speed up or slow down the beat. The thought occurred to me that I might be hitting the bass drum on the up beat and the snare drum on the down beat. Who would know the difference? The show seemed to be going very well despite my not knowing.

Halfway through the song, although it could barely be heard above the roar of the excited crowd, my left leg seemed to be stretched to its limit as I tried to press down on the foot pedal. I continued without hesitation to pound out the rhythmic, primitive jungle beat of America's number one song. Then I realized I had not hit the cymbal on the eighth beat for awhile and immediately attempted a vicious shot. Every time I stomped down the foot pedal, the bass drum moved slightly across the slick hardwood floor. There was no time to stop whacking away and attempt to pull it back. I didn't want to lose the beat and throw the band off. I'd have to slink down in my folding chair and extend my foot far out for the foot pedal, hit the snare drum and occasionally bang the cymbal. Maybe the song would end before the drum fell over the edge of the stage. Unfortunately, slunk down like that in the chair, I could not easily reach the cymbal and had to exert a sudden physical lunge over the top of the snare drum, missing the first time but quickly trying again assuming we were within two, maybe three beats of that eighth one they talked about.

Finally, the song ended...one artist at a time. Since I couldn't hear them wrap it up, and I was watching Mrs. Ann gasping for her breath, I continued to hit the snare on one beat and flail a stick at the cymbal whenever the mood struck. The bass was too far away to even try. Someone tapped me on the shoulder. It was Joe.

"We're done," he said. "You can stop now."

Thank God. The bass was halfway up the aisle. I had lost my place anyway. The curtain closed. For what seemed like a long time, a screaming roar of applause vibrated against the big blue felt curtain.

The Hidden Power of a Mother

You're crazy if you think I care. Nobody will ever know it 100 years from now anyway so if you think I give a crap what they think of me you've got another think coming. I know what's important in life and I can tell you right now it's not grades. Some of them have been working their butts off their entire lives just to have someone scratch an "A" on a piece of paper so they can show it to their sweet Mommie and get a cookie for their trouble. I say to hell with that.

Next year the major league scouts will be all over me just like Fishhook. The Cardinals will offer me a professional contract and I'll sign that thing so fast it'll make your head swim, man. I'll come back to Greenwood and drive out to the Tastee Freeze in a new Cadillac convertible, then I'll open a restaurant, a fancy one and I'll wear a tux at the door and sit at the bar like Humphrey Bogart and when people come in I'll sign autographs.

So, anyway, maybe I should read that story about the wolf or whatever the hell that is. Mrs. Ann is such a nag about homework. Jeez! Doesn't she get it? I don't need to memorize the Canterbury Tales. I can just see it now, old Diz interviewing me after I pitch a no-hitter in the World Series and everyone is screaming and the cameras are on me and I'm sweating and they're pouring champagne over my head and old Diz says, "What a game you pitched out there tonight, Podnah. No hits, no runs, struck out 17 and no walks. Now, can you quote just a little bit of them Canterbury Tales for me?"

"James, what are you doing?" It was Mama calling from the kitchen trying to do her motherly duty toward her problem son.

"Nothin'," I said as I lay on the bed tossing a baseball toward the ceiling and catching it in my glove.

"Do you have any homework?"

"Huhhhhhh. Well, supposed to read a story of some kind and write a report for English lit."

"Got your book here?"

"I think so."

She poked her head in the doorway and with a cheerful voice tried to get me interested in the story. I had read many stories the last few years. *Bonus Baby, Robinson Crusoe, Last of the Mohicans,* and the one about Michelangelo and how he painted the Sistine Chapel ceiling. Stories about people who had just one single thing their whole life revolved around. Like the *Bonus Baby* had only one thing in his life. His fastball. Someday I hoped I would do just one thing better than anybody else on the whole planet. The *Bonus Baby* or Michelangelo didn't worry about writing a report on the *Canterbury Tales;* they didn't worry about their driver's license, or a date, or going to the dentist, or what the other kids think of them, or going to hell or heaven, or college. , or getting a job or anything like that. Did Lance Alworth worry about English Lit? I doubt it!

"So, what's the story?" she asked casually as I tossed the ball up to the ceiling.

"Something about a wolf."

"Beowulf?"

"Something like that."

"Hon, Beowulf is not about a wolf."

My mother seemed to know everything. You could name just about anything and Mom would know something about it. And she thought everything was good.

"Hon, it's really good."

See. Did I tell you?

"So, what's good about it?" I asked, still tossing the baseball up to the ceiling.

"It's about a warrior," she said as she entered the room and sat down on the bed beside me. "He came from a far off land to Denmark to do battle with a monster who had been killing the King's finest soldiers for 10 years. The warrior's name was Beowulf and he had a great reputation like John Wayne."

"Mom, please. You don't have to throw in contemporary lingo like they do at church so the young people won't be bored. Give me a break."

"Sorry. Beowulf and his soldiers arrived at the castle and had a big party with food and music and poetry readings and beer and...."

"They had beer in those days?"

"Yes, but they called it mead or ale or something. And they had a bragging contest to extol the — "

"What's extol?"

"Brag or pronounce the virtues of this visiting warrior. Beowulf gave a speech about how great he was and that he was so fierce in battle that he would not need his shield or sword when he fought. The monster was Grendel. He was like a spirit monster from the deep earth or from some dark place. Anyway, Beowulf said he'd take on the monster with his bare hands."

"That's a little like David and Goliath."

"Yes, it is. You know I hadn't thought of the comparison but it is similar."

"So what happened?"

"Don't you want to read it?"

"I don't know yet. Tell me what happened and I'll see."

"Good trick, get me to tell it and you won't have to read it."

"Go ahead."

"Well, the monster shows up at the banquet hall very late at night after they are all asleep and kills one or two warriors in their sleep and eats them."

"Oh, my Lord!"

"It's pretty gory stuff."

"Mama, when did you read this story?"

"Two years ago in summer school. Remember when I was driving up to the University every day? I had a literature class."

It seemed like forever during the summer months Mama drove 80 miles to Fayetteville each day to maintain her teaching certificate. During those weeks she became very tired and irritable. Her hair was graying at the temples and lines had formed on her face. She mumbled to herself in the kitchen and sometimes banged pots and pans in anger. One day I walked in the front door arriving early from the baseball field and heard her crying in her bedroom. I hurried in and sat on the edge of her bed and asked her what was wrong. She quit crying and smiled at me and said, "Nothing, hon, I'm just tired."

"Then the monster, Grendel, comes to Beowulf who does not sleep, remember that others had fallen asleep and were killed probably because they were drunk. But Beowulf was wide awake. So there was a tremendous battle of strength. Beowulf is so strong that he won't let go of the monster who realizes he is in a serious battle. It's like a wrestling match."

"Like the Great Bolo and Oni Wiki-Wiki at Jimmy Lott's Sports Arena at 210 Towson Avenue right here in Fort Smith," I said mimicking the sound of Jimmy Lott who advertised his professional wrestling matches on TV every Wednesday night. Suddenly she was young again with laughter. "Right! Just like those wrestling matches, and you do that so well, that's funny!"

"OK so, anyway," she continued the story, "the monster pulls away from Beowulf who tears the monster's arm and shoulder off in the process."

"Gross, man!"

"Yes, it's all bloody and gory. The monster kills the men and eats them or drags them back to his cave."

"So, does he die?"

"Well, yes, he does and then it gets really interesting. The next night they celebrate the defeat of Grendel, have a big party. That very night guess who shows up and kills several of the King's favorite warriors?"

"Grendel?"

"Nope."

"I don't know. Who?"

"Grendel's mother."

"What?"

"Grendel's mother who is also a spirit-monster seeks revenge for the death of her son and shows up and kills and devours some men and goes back to her cave in the depths of an underworld cave lake."

"Now wait a minute. Grendel's mother?"

"Yep. It turns out that the real problem was the mother. In class we talked about how the mother was a symbol in this old story."

"What kind of symbol?"

"Well, you know, like the source of the problem reappears in the stillness of sleep or dreams."

"Oh. Then what happens?"

"Beowulf sets out to find Grendel's mother and goes under the lake into her cave. There is a fierce battle and Beowulf almost gets killed when his sword breaks. But suddenly he sees a huge ancient sword in the corner, a famous sword, grabs it, and quickly cuts of the head of Grendel's mother."

"Jeez!"

"Don't say that, hon."

"Wow!"

"Pretty good story, huh?" She walked out the door into the kitchen.

"Yeah."

"Oh, I almost forgot," she said as her face appeared in the doorway suddenly animated with eyes sparkling. "A very big part of the story was why Beowulf fought the monsters."

"Why did he?"

"At the very end of the story, the last sentence, the last line, it says that Beowulf was 'most eager for fame.'"

"What do you mean?"

"In that period, the 10th century, they weren't too informed about eternal life, so for a warrior to be remembered, to leave a legend or a legacy, was the next best thing to eternal life."

"So?"

"So, it's OK to want to do something big to be remembered. It's natural to want to be a famous ball player or to find fame."

"Oh."

"You just have to find your own way."

My mother was really smart.

I couldn't imagine reading the story and writing a report. It was too much. Everything seemed so hard.

"Oh, hon," Mama stuck her head back in the door.

"Yeah."

"Mrs. Ann said the report could be an oral report. You have to do it by Friday."

An oral report? Maybe I could do that. Maybe I could tell the story just like she had told it to me. As smart as she was, Mama didn't know why Beowulf was read in class in little towns in Arkansas in 1962.

On Friday I walked to the front of the class filled with mostly seniors and told the story of Beowulf. The class seemed interested and watched and listened. They laughed when I described the party scene in the mead hall and they became very quiet when I told about the final battle between Beowulf and Grendel's mother. I wasn't nervous at all and felt myself enjoying, relishing the oral storytelling. I was good and knew it. I sat down. The class applauded. And my life changed courses that day, in that very moment.

Mrs. Ann asked me to stay after class. I stood at her desk. Mrs. Ann looked at me through steel gray eyes.

"James," she said, "that was very good."

"Thanks."

"You should do more of that."

At the end of the semester I received an "A" in English literature. It is the only "A" on my high school transcript. I guess you could say old Grendel and I had very strong mothers.

PART II
Second Childhood

.

Photos

The Farm, circa 1940, near Milltown, Arkansas.

Coach Grady Robinson delivers his humorous speech at the football banquet at Whaley's Cafe in 1950.

(left) Daddy holds David, Mama holds me on the front steps of the farm on Easter Day 1946. Jane was not born until 1951.

(below left) Wilma Hill Robinson was not only beautiful, she was also voted class clown at Alma High School in 1933-34.

(below right) This is the father I remember most from 1960 when I was trying to become a Lance Alworth for him.

(top) Me about nine years old. One year after getting beaned by Fishhook.

(right) Sophomore quarterback James Robinson hands off to Joe Stafford, 1960. Joe and I played football, basketball and baseball together throughout childhood.

(below) My one-room office high above Spencer's Grill in Kirkwood where I launched into stand-up comedy and a writing career, 1981.

Slugger Ryan faces the Gooden Machine in Kirkwood Little League, 1984.

(above) Ryan at Busch Stadium on the day his old man gives it one last shot to redeem himself at the Randy Hundley Fantasy Baseball Camp. That day I pitched against Bob Gibson, Curt Flood, Joe Cunningham and Randy Hundley.

(left) Ryan graduates *cum laude* from Boston College, 1999.

Opening Night

I threw the first warm-up pitch of the 1964 baseball season. The ball sailed through the air, grew smaller in an instant and slammed into the catcher's mitt. A puff of dust surrounded the mitt, and the catcher fired the ball back to the mound.

I glanced up into the stands of Hunts Park and saw Kansas City scout Whitey Herzog watching me warm up. There is no sound on earth more exciting than that of the blazing fastball and the hiss, swoosh and boom of the mitt. "You can teach a kid to pitch," my dad said, "but a fastball is a God-given gift." It had finally happened. Between my sophomore and junior year in high school, I had sprouted up to 6'3". God had seen fit to smile down on my right arm.

I wound up again, and on the second warm up pitch, turned it up a notch. On game night the adrenaline flowed and the fastball seemed to explode out of my hand and disappear with a hiss toward the plate. Under the lights, the white ball looked like a laser beam, a streak of hot lava. I was finally there after all those years of watching the big boys, being the little guy, being second to my brother David, and Daddy ignoring me. I was standing out here with a gift from God, the fastball I had always dreamed of. Just that one thing was all a man needed.

The game that night was against a top Legion team sponsored by Vehicle, a Fort Smith hardware store, and the team was managed by Shelby "The Duke" Breedlove, my basketball and baseball coach at Fort Smith Junior College.

The catcher tossed the ball back and I adjusted my belt and spit a stream of Red Man tobacco on the mound staking my claim to the hill. "Bring 'em on dammit!" I mumbled out loud, trying to act mean. I strutted and snorted like a warrior.

I looked good. I felt good. I had become a man. I was Lance Alworth.

Doubts about my sore right shoulder had been haunting me for weeks, and I had prayed to God for a healing. There I stood with the gift that only God could give, the live arm, the blazing fastball; and yet one torn muscle or a blown rotator cuff blown, and all those years of longing for major league fame and total approval of my father and brother would go up in smoke.

A slower, smoother follow through would lessen the strain on my shoulder. In the seconds before the first pitch, I made a decision. I would hold back just a little and hope that any balls hit would be caught by my defense. There was no need to throw too hard and strain it again.

I would slow everything down, plant my left foot and then bring my shoulder and arm around with a smooth move that I hoped would not put too much strain on the shoulder. The catcher trotted to the mound to get our signals straight. One finger for fast ball, two for my weakass curve that served as a change-up because it didn't curve much. But who needed a curve when you've got the gift from God? Such an unimportant detail. That one thing was all I needed.

"Cole, how's it moving?"

"Real good, man. The ball is hopping and fast."

"Really, are you sure? I'm slowing down my motion to be certain I don't strain this damn shoulder again."

"You just keep up whatever you were doing because it's humming in there strong."

Five of the opposing players had played with me on the junior college team. They knew my bad habits. They knew I threw a good fastball and they also knew I was wild. They knew I'd lose my temper the first time a call didn't go my way. I anticipated vicious razzing from their dugout. The bench jockeys would ride me hard and be certain to remind me of the nickname I hated, Gomer. My silly imitation of Gomer Pyle had stuck.

The first batter walked to the plate, Cotton Nye, a crafty little second baseman, lead-off man for the college team and a good buddy.

"OK, James," I said to myself, "just throw strikes if you can. Slow the windup, relax and follow through with a slow flowing motion so the arm doesn't jerk to a stop and strain the torn muscle."

Mama and Daddy were watching on the grassy hillside from their lawn chairs with a few hundred fans. A thermos jug filled with ice water sat beside Daddy as he nervously smoked one cigarette after another. They watched as I went into my windup. I brought the glove and ball over my head in the traditional pitcher's style with the left leg kicked into the air and my foot thrust toward home plate. I planted my foot more carefully than usual, concentrating on a smooth motion; and then, instead of firing my arm around as fast as I could hoping the ball would go somewhere near the plate, I relaxed and followed through all the way to the ground. The ball left my hand and grew smaller, humming toward the plate, the catcher and the batter. The ball flew right down the middle, slammed into the mitt, and the umpire, Chesty Foster, growled, "Steee-riiike."

Strike one and a long way to go. I adjusted my cap and kicked at the rubber in the traditional pitcher ritual and enjoyed the cheers from my own bench and the chatter from my infield. Once again, I went into the windup being very careful to slow everything down. The ball seemed to leap from my hand and then accelerate as it moved toward the plate. It was going right down the middle for the second straight time. Cotton swung. The ball had already slammed into the mitt making an unusually loud smack into the glove. My infield yelled encouragement, a few fans applauded and the Vehicle dugout was already into their taunts and insults.

"Don't worry, Cotton. He can't throw three in a row. Get ready to duck!"

"Hey, Gomer, is that you?"

"You sure you didn't send your big brother?" They died laughing.

That pissed me off.

"Yeah, big brother this, you cockroaches!" I wound up, sucked up some energy, and fired another one as hard as I could and the ball zoomed high over the catcher and hit the backstop ten feet up. Their bench went wild. I stepped back off the mound to think. It was not complicated. The first two pitches with the slower motion were perfect strikes. The third pitch I threw too hard out of anger, and it went over the moon. "James, that's exactly what they want. Stay calm and deliberate. Slow it down!" I picked up the resin bag, spat on the mound and glanced toward Whitey Herzog and the other major league scouts.

I stepped back on the rubber. Take the sign. Fastball. Good. It's the only pitch I've got anyway. But wait now, back off a little, slow and smooth. Hsst, boom!

"Steee-riiike," Chesty Foster's voice split the air.

Through the first, second and third innings, I threw with ease and control. The scoreboard showed no runs, no hits, no errors and more importantly, no walks. Something magical and wonderful was happening to me. Inning after inning I walked to the mound in a dream-like state. The shoulder had twinged twice but not bad. It had only reminded me to go back to slow, smooth-flowing rhythm.

The ball seemed to leave my hand and, as if on a laser beam, sizzled toward the plate, moving slightly inside and outside by some kind of telepathy: low and outside when I think about it, high and inside without aiming.

It was a masterful pitching performance. A one-hitter, 16 strikeouts, no walks, a shutout. People swarmed me with pats on the back, and extending their hand offered congratulations. The guys on the other team were gushing in their compliments when we chatted after the game. Coach Breedlove approached me. "Helluva game, Gomer. I always knew that was in you. You really showed me something out there tonight."

"Thank you, Coach." I had never felt more alive and happy. To have Coach Breedlove's respect was deeply important to me.

We piled in the car for the half hour ride back to Greenwood. I couldn't wait to hear what Daddy would say about such an athletic achievement. David had pitched no-hitters before — one as an eight year old, another as an all-AIC pitcher for Arkansas Tech — and had often won crucial games with gutsy and brilliant pitching performances in high school, college and American Legion. He would win many more big ones in the next few years in semi-pro baseball. I had always shown tremendous potential with my live arm and actually threw harder than David. But for reasons that I would not understand until later in life, I seldom had the success in sports that David enjoyed. The real success was always just beyond my reach. But on that night it had finally happened, I had stolen the show and was the dominant figure of the night.

We sat in silence as the car drove down old Greenwood Road toward Highway 71. I decided I would not be the first to speak. If he wanted to be silent, let him. I'm not going to beg for approval. I'm not going to act like an immature kid and say something like, "Gee, Dad, didja see that? Huh?"

Coach Grady was driving. One word from him could bring the blessing I so desperately needed. Maybe I could never be a Lance Alworth. But being me would be enough. Mama was seated in the back seat. She grew a little uneasy with the strange silence when, in a rare moment, Daddy could have been effusive in his compliments. We drove for a while. Finally, she couldn't bear it any longer.

Hoping my father would give me the approval she knew I longed for, she said, "Well, Grady, what did you think of James's performance?"

He said, "Well, pretty good but he'll never do it again."

I woke up the next morning and walked to town to read the sports page and get my breakfast of Pepsi and peanuts. My arm was stiff, but I had not reinjured the shoulder and was relieved. Mama had gasped when he said that. I was so stunned that I just sat there and thought about those words and why he said such a thing. "He'll never do it again."

I walked into Dawson's store and pulled the Pepsi out of the machine and the sack of peanuts off the rack. "Charge it, Alec."

"Your picture is in the paper this morning," Alec mumbled as he wrote the charge of twenty cents down on the Robinson account.

I opened the *Southwest American* to the sports page. The headlines read in large letters, "One-Hitter ushers in Legion season." My picture appeared in the column below. "James Robinson fired a one-hitter and Mike Perkins supplied the big bat as Midwest thumped the Vehicle nine, 8-0 last night at Hunts Park to open the local American Legion season. Robinson was untouchable except for a triple by Vehicle outfielder Jimmy Pogue. Vehicle loser Butch Edwards, a Fort

Smith Junior College teammate of Robinson, was effective but a leaky defense cost him."

I turned the bottle upside down, watched the peanuts float back upward and enjoyed breakfast. I looked at the picture.

The phrase, "He'll never do it again," seemed to hang in the air. I was pondering those words and feeling uneasy. Maybe the game last night was pure luck. Maybe I can never do it again. Even if it was true, how could a father allow such a statement to come out of his mouth? Mama had almost fainted and had said, "Grady, for crying out loud, what do you mean?" He knew immediately that he was in serious trouble and should not have said such a thing. He tried to smooth it over by saying something like, "Well, I mean, everything went his way and you don't normally get all the calls...." But I knew he meant something more ominous and she knew that too. She collapsed back in her seat, "For crying out loud, Grady!"

I walked out the door of the grocery store and headed down the street toward the library where I would peruse the shelves and read in the cool air of the court house basement. It was a beautiful summer morning. Mr. Stafford's cleaners was hissing steam as usual with the white puffs flowing through the narrow opening between his building and the *Greenwood Democrat*. He waved out the window and yelled across the street, "Helluva game last night, James."

"Thanks," I waved back.

"You're on your way now! Helluva game!"

Mr. Ward was in his shoe shop. Suddenly his head appeared at the door. Mr. Ward was not known for small talk. He devoted every moment of the day to the cutting of shoe leather, the pounding of tiny nails with the flat-nosed hammer and the polishing of repaired shoes. He spoke with a tight lip that seemed to begrudge any demand for words. "You must have put on quite a show last night," he said as he worked the inside of a shoe while standing at the door.

"I got lucky I guess."

"Willard said you were throwing a major league fastball and hittin' the corners with it."

"I threw pretty good. Seemed to have control and the ball was moving sideways too."

"Keep it up. We might have somebody from this town play in the major leagues yet."

Not since Mr. Ward's uncle, Aaron Ward, played for the Yankees in 1922 had a favorite son played in the major leagues. If I could make it to the major leagues, I would prove to my father...but he was probably right. He knew ball players. He was the coach and he had said as plain as day, "He'll never do it again."

He was wrong.

Never Enough

It was late when I heard Mama and Daddy talking softly in their room. Jane and Momaw were asleep. Then I heard Mama talking on the phone. I got up and walked to the kitchen door.

"Something wrong?"

"He's still not feeling well," she said into the receiver. Her tone was a familiar one, filled with strength and resolve.

There was silence as she listened to Dr. Bailey. Then she spoke.

"He has some pain in his left arm and he's not breathing well."

I walked across the living room and approached their bedroom. Daddy lay on his side. I entered the room and asked him what was wrong.

"Oh, nothing," he growled. "Probably an ulcer after the God-awful football season we had. But your Mama's worried about my heart and called Doc Bailey."

I didn't know what to say. He had never been sick before.

Mama hung up the phone and walked back into the room. "Dr. Bailey is going to call Bud Corbin. They'll be up in a little while with the ambulance and we're going to the hospital emergency room."

"Now, Wilma," he began.

"Grady, don't even start. We're going to have you looked at and that's final."

The next day I walked down the corridor of St. Edward's Hospital. Lunch trays were stacked on a cart. The unpleasant hospital smell filled the hallways and the food on the trays looked dry and tasteless. I asked the nurse what room he was in and she pointed down the hallway and smiled. "He's a pistol, that Grady." Daddy had already charmed the nurses with innocent flirting and complaining about not being able to smoke a cigarette. He was sitting up in bed and looked fine. The flattop haircut seemed to accentuate the streaks of gray appearing at his temples. The TV was on and Bill Cullen emceed a day time game show, "The Price Is Right." We watched it every day during the summer just before baseball practice.

"Hey, Hoss!" he said.

"How you feeling?"

"Fine."

A monkey blew a horn on "The Price Is Right" as Bill Cullen quizzed a contestant about the price of a set of luggage.

"Yep. I'm feeling fine," he said.

"Well, what did they say?"

"The Doc said it might have been a little heart flare up or it might not."

"So what does that mean? You OK or not?"

"I'll be fine," he said. "Said I gotta quit smoking."

We both knew he couldn't or wouldn't quit smoking. I wanted to tell him how worried I was but didn't dare say anything like that. Such a straightforward statement would have made him very uncomfortable. I sat in a chair and watched TV.

Daddy had never been sick before. I could not remember seeing him sick, incapacitated or in pain. The day he had his teeth pulled by Dr. Tynt Graham in Van Buren, Ark., we drove back to Greenwood, David, Jane and me in the back seat of the car, with Dad driving. Mama wanted to drive but he said he was fine and could drive even though Doc Graham had pulled most of his teeth in preparation for dentures. At the stoplight in Van Buren he opened the car door and leaned out the car and spit blood onto the pavement. There was a puddle of bright red blood on the pavement. We drove away.

He lay in the hospital bed quietly watching the TV. His leathery tanned skin seemed even more tan against the white sheets. He was 54 years old and had gained weight. His stomach was big and he had changed dramatically from his youthful days of athletics when he was tall and thin with wavy black hair.

We watched "The Price Is Right" in silence. Finally he spoke.

"You boys got a game tonight?"

"Yeah. We play Southern Baptist from Walnut Ridge."

"They beat you down there didn't they?"

"Yeah. We were awful down there."

"You boys have improved a lot. You'll likely beat 'em here at home." He seemed to know something. I played basketball at Fort Smith Junior College. After a mediocre senior year at Greenwood I had surprisingly received a basketball-baseball scholarship at Fort Smith Junior College. My freshman year was uneventful. But by my sophomore year, Coach Breedlove placed me in the starting lineup at forward on the Lion basketball team. I had improved some and because I was tall and could run fast and jump I was placed in the starting lineup.

"Maybe. I think we can," I said.

Silence. The monkey blew the horn again. The audience laughed.

"Is Mama coming up?" I asked.

"She'll be here after school."

"You be OK for a while?"

"Oh, yeah. Got my TV and some green Jell-O. No coffee, no sweets, no fried food, no cigarettes. How's that for living high?" he said with dry sarcasm.

"I've got to go to a pre-game workout."

"That's fine. I'll be listening on the radio tonight."

"OK."

"Bye."

"Bye, son. Play good."

"OK."

I wanted to touch him. I wanted to hug him or something, but it just didn't seem appropriate. I wanted to tell him I loved him. I wanted him to tell me that he loved me. The words hung in my throat.

"So, OK," I said at the door, "You're all set here, right?"

"Oh, yeah! I'm fine."

"OK, great. I'll see you tomorrow."

I walked down the corridor feeling empty and a little frightened. It was strange to see him lying in a hospital bed in a green gown. I had never thought of him not being healthy, vibrant, bigger than life and always there. I knew he loved me. "Bye, son, play good," was a nice thing for him to say.

I felt him trying to be close to me in the tone of his voice. Why was I so nervous in his presence? I guess it was the fact that he was in bed, sick, lying down that had caused such unease in me. Then as I drove to the Wheeler Boys Club gym for our pre-game shootaround, it suddenly dawned on me: we had never before had a one-on-one conversation. Seldom since early childhood could I recall being alone with him in a conversation and never a conversation that was not about sports or something related to sports. He was my father and much of my whole life had been shaped around his presence, and yet we had not had a single conversation.

We played almost forty games that season. After a dozen games or so I began to rebound very well and had learned to play tough defense. In the *Fort Smith Times Record,* sports columnist Jesse Owens quoted Coach Breedlove:

>...this year's team has made more progress than any other. Freshman Philip Hoffman and James Bridges have been the nucleus of the team. But the real progress has been turned in by Larry Bunch, Butch Edwards and James Robinson. Robinson has been a living terror during a nine game stretch when the Lions won six and lost three. In a game against John Brown University we pulled out a 93-85 win due to the "rebounding of Larry Bunch and James Robinson."

Under a picture of me in the *Southwest-Times Record* shooting a jump shot against Oklahoma City University, the caption read, "High Flying Lion, James Robinson of Fort Smith Junior College leaps high over a defender."

That night against Southern Baptist, with Daddy listening on the radio from his hospital bed, I pulled down 13 rebounds in the first half. During the second half I grabbed six more, and with three minutes left in the game got two more. Suddenly all the fans were cheering me on. I didn't know why. Every time the ball went up I took two steps toward the bucket and jumped as high as I could. If the ball went through the hoop I simply landed and went back down the floor. But if the ball caromed off the rim or backboard I was already airborne and ripped it off the boards with just a little too much flair. I was not a great player. But I was tall, 6'5", and I could jump. That night the ball came my way. I went up and there it was, got it. With three minutes to go in the game James Bridges shot from the corner and it rimmed out. I went up and grabbed the rebound and heard everyone yelling. I had broken the single game rebound record with 21.

The next morning the headlines read "JC Lions Nip Baptist."

> Holding a narrow 41-39 lead at the half behind the outstanding shooting and recordbreaking rebounding of James Robinson, the Lions came out cold to start the second half missing their first nine shots before Robinson finally connected.... Robinson racked the boards clean time after time and finished with a grand total of 21 for the new mark. Robinson finished the game with 21 points and 21 rebounds.

At the bottom of the sports page that day there was a personal note from the sports page editor:

> A Get Well greeting to Grady Robinson. Greenwood's Dean of District 4-A Coaches is in St. Edwards Hospital. He went in for a checkup on chest pains and they found a small ulcer. And that seems logical. Coaches just aren't in these days unless they have an ulcer. Robinson, who is scheduled to return home Monday, said, "After the football season we had, I'm lucky it's a small one."

Dad got out of the hospital. The prognosis was positive. He had had a slight heart attack but the doctor assured him that if he would quit smoking, stop eating fried foods and exercise, he would live a long, healthy life. Naturally, he didn't change one aspect of his personal habits.

A few weeks later I played in my last game for the Fort Smith Junior College Lions against the University of Arkansas freshmen. The Hogs always drew a big crowd even if it was only the freshmen. The Southside High gym was packed, including Elaine Gage, a preacher's daughter who could sing like Barbra Streisand. At every time-out while Coach Breedlove was giving instructions, I was winking and smiling at the gorgeous Elaine. Coach B went nuts. "Gomer! Who in the hell are you lookin' at? Get your head in the game!" It was a very close game. With fifteen seconds left in the game and the score tied, I cut off a pass and stole the ball. The place went nuts. I was flying down the court concentrating on the dribble. For reasons beyond explanation I decided to veer by the area where the lovely Miss Gage had refused to acknowledge my glances. As I roared by the bench, and I looked over her way to locate her hazel eyes I heard Coach Breedlove, a devout Christian who rarely took the Lord's name in vain, screaming, "*#^!&# you, Gomer! Take it in, for God's sake!" I saw Elaine and smiled, somehow maintained the dribble and kept the Hog defenders on my tail. I thought about a slam dunk to close out my career at Fort Smith. A slam dunk or play it safe, make the easy lay-up for the team. Personal glory or a win for the team? I went up high over the rim, paused, and then laid the ball softly against the glass. The crowd roared. I scored 22 points and grabbed 17 rebounds. It was my last game at Fort Smith Junior College.

After playing only one year of high school basketball I closed out my junior college career as the leading rebounder with 321. Scored 311 points, made 49 free throws.

On the way home that night, Dad sat in the back seat with Mama.

I waited for the word. David said, "Good game," Mama said, "James, that was great! What a way to close the season!"

I waited. There was silence as Daddy blew the cigarette smoke out the window.

Then he said, "Why didn't you dunk that lay-up?"

A Thanksgiving Day Football

"Hut one! Hut two!" I barked, licking the salty remains of turkey from my lips just as the football came flying toward me. Overweight, potbellied grown men in full pads snorted and grunted, trying to block my punt. I, too, was suited up in a complete football uniform, looking through the face mask of a helmet that smelled of sweat-stained padding. As our opponents, the Mansfield (Ark.) High School alumni, charged, through a blur of red and blue, I suddenly realized I didn't want to punt. I tucked the football under my arm and ran with all haste to the left.

I was doing what almost every armchair athlete dreams of as he looks back on his high school football career — giving it another shot. He's thinking, "Why wasn't I better? Why wasn't I a star?" At age 22 or 32 he's 20 pounds heavier than he was as a 17-year-old fuzzy-cheeked high-schooler. Because he is older, he is also tougher and more aggressive, and thus, quite naturally, he looks back and wonders, "Why wasn't I meaner, tougher, and faster?"

Many of us would give a month's salary for one more chance, and that's why the Greenwood Bulldogs vs. the

Mansfield Tigers alumni game came about on Thanksgiving Day 1973. It was publicized as a fund-raising event for the Jaycees, but that was obviously just a cover. The oldtimers wanted another crack at the gridiron and were willing to risk life, limb and gainful employment to prove to the world, to the town, to family and friends, and mostly to themselves, that they were indeed, or perhaps could have been, Lance Alworth.

My wife and I had driven the 200 miles to Greenwood from our home in Tulsa to share Thanksgiving dinner with my family. I was stiff and sleepy as we drove by the school headed north on Main Street. Then I had noticed the hundreds of cars parked at the football field. I straightened up, alert and wondering who might be playing. We pulled into the driveway of the home where I spent my youth fantasizing about athletic greatness and being a Lance Alworth-like hero or a Stan Musial or Mickey Mantle. We got out of the car, and I could see from our front yard that there was an alumni game and tried to remember if I had brought any sweat socks.

Dad had coached for 38 years and had retired the year before. We greeted each other at the front door. "Hi, Mom! Hi, Dad! Say, what's going on down at the field?" I asked as I gave my mom a warm hug and, as usual, avoided physical contact with Dad.

"Those crazy Jaycees have an old-timers game going," my father growled. "It's insane. Out of shape, overweight, they'll kill each other."

"Yeah, it's really stupid," I agreed, peeping out the window. "What are they trying to prove? Get a life, huh?"

"I should hope so," a voice rang out from the kitchen, where my mother pulled the turkey and dressing from the oven. "The last time you got in an alumni game you spent the night in the hospital, remember?"

"Yeah," I said, and laughed, too loudly. "That was just one of those things. Accidents happen."

"Lots of accidents that night. If I remember correctly, four of you ended up in the hospital."

"What on earth did you do?" asked my wife, Armetta, who had never heard of the alumni game seven years earlier, when we played the Air National Guard of Fort Smith. It seemed like half the town had ended up hospitalized or immobilized, but we won 19-6.

"Collarbone, no problem, actually. Say, when do we eat?"

"It's ready right now."

We had a wonderful Thanksgiving dinner with all the trimmings. The talk was good and it was nice to be with the family. I enjoyed the home cooking, but I began to get restless. After the main course I said, "Hey, I think I'll walk down to the field and see some of the old gang, and then after the game, I'll come back for pumpkin pie."

"OK, fine," said Mom. "I'll have it ready with fresh coffee."

Dad gave me a strange look, but I walked nonchalantly out the back door. After I closed it, I sprinted for the car, and frantically dug out the sweat socks.

I arrived just before the half and took a seat in the stands, where I chatted with people I had known in high school. The players on the field looked slow and overweight. Plumbers, truck drivers, salesmen and a few coaches were out there together like big prize hogs at the fair. The rules permitted unlimited substitutions and time-outs.

At the half I walked into the locker room and greeted old friends. We laughed and joked a bit.

"Hey, Robinson, git it on. Here's some shoes," said Gary Gilliam, president of the class of 1963 and left tackle on the 8-2 Bulldogs.

"Oh, man! You got to be kidding," I said as I scanned the room for some shoulder pads and pants. "I'm too old for that stuff. You guys are crazy."

"Sure we are, but I got in one lick that made it all worth it."

"Yeah, it's crazy," said Charlie Miller, a long-time pal, "but whoever said we was smart?" We all laughed.

By the end of the halftime break the wild stories were finished, the beer all gone, and I had my entire uniform picked out. As the battered players walked out to the field, I quickly peeled off my shirt and pants and slipped on the sweat socks. I pulled on football pants and stuffed two very cold thigh pads into the pockets inside the pants. I luckily found shoes that fit on the first try, pulled on shoulder pads and grabbed a jersey that had been lying on the floor. No. 25. The third helmet I tried on fit perfectly, and at the kickoff, I walked to the Greenwood bench, feeling like an idiot.

"Well, look what the dogs drug up, boys," someone said.

Halfway through the third quarter, the Bulldogs had failed to move the ball. "We need a punter," someone shouted.

"I'll try it!" I chirped. I had punted in high school just 10 seasons earlier.

"Get in there and punt."

So that's how it happened. Full of turkey and dressing and gravy and yams and hot rolls, 27 years old, a family to support, a tender body, and two 240-pounders coming directly at me with bodily harm in mind.

I tucked the football and sprinted left. It took them by surprise and the field was wide open. I ran for 35 yards before the opposition began to close in. The run was euphoric. I tried to fake left and go right, but the fake didn't take and I was hit from four directions. Luckily, no one got in a solid blow, and I came down with only a busted lip that puffed up like an old bike tire. I came off the field to the roar of the crowd — a few wives and kids.

We laughed. We hollered at each other and laughed some more and cussed and complained and wiped traces of blood from noses and lips.

In the fourth quarter, the Mansfield alumni led 6-0; it was a game filled with defensive brilliance. Also, everyone ran in slow motion. We had a third and six on our 43-yard line and someone said, "Put Robinson in there, he used to throw."

There I stood again, now under the center. We had decided to sweep left. I would simply hand the ball to Carroll Lowe, one of the great Bulldog halfbacks of all time, from the class of '66. "Hut one," I roared, hoping my voice wouldn't be recognized echoing up the hill 200 yards to our house. "Hut two," and the ball slapped firmly into my hands. I stepped back and, just as I had 10 years earlier, I held the ball out for the half-back — but this time something strange happened. Maybe it was because I subconsciously felt that as a high school athlete I had been a disappointment to my father, or maybe it was because in high school we had run the single wing and as the quarterback I seldom got to carry the ball. Or maybe it was because after high school I ran track in college and after five years of hard work could run a 100-yard dash under 10 seconds even though it took me 30 yards to get my long frame unwound out of the blocks. Who knows why I faked the ball and ran a naked bootleg around right end?

It was an interesting experience. My stomach was still full of turkey, and when I circled right end I saw that two men in red helmets were coming my way. That's when I thought, "This is insane."

I tried to relax and run. I saw they were overweight. I figured them for a coalminer and a factory worker who liked to deer hunt. I got unwound. They snorted and moaned. I heard them breathing heavy. I burped. I went down the sideline untouched. At the 10-yard line I looked up to the chain fence and saw the silhouette of a large man with a flat top haircut. He stood there watching, smoking a cigarette.

More laughter on the bench. More headshaking and bad jokes about aging, and slaps on the back and a funny feeling inside my stomach. It's not every Thanksgiving that I make a 67-yard touchdown run.

After the game, which we won 12-6, I quickly dressed, shouted a goodbye to old friends and was out the door in five minutes. I jogged back to the house, walked through the door and sat down at the table just in time to get some pumpkin pie and fresh coffee.

"Who won?" asked Mother, to make conversation.

"Oh, I think Greenwood did," I said.

"See anybody you know?" asked Dad calmly.

"Oh sure, the whole bunch. Crazy guys were having a ball."

"Say," said Dad with a sarcastic grin, "who was the big ol' tall boy down there?"

"Just an oldtimer come back to recapture his youth," I replied. "Some poor old boy trying one more time to prove he's a Lance Alworth."

My wife said, "What's wrong with your lip?"

World Series Tickets

"We've got one last chance," I mumbled to Kenny Kaaiohelo, my old college pal, who had just driven 10 hours and 500 miles from Edmond, Okla., with his two sons, Jason and Jared, to see the sixth game of the 1982 World Series in St. Louis.

"What's that?" Kenny asked, flashing his Hawaiian smile, trying to remain chipper and upbeat about my not being able to come up with the tickets I'd promised.

I glanced at the Goodyear Blimp hanging above Busch Stadium. Even its drone as it fought the strong winds seemed to be a growl directed at me.

Jason, 12, and Jared, 10, apparently unconcerned about our lack of tickets, talked excitedly as we walked past NBC equipment trucks, souvenir vendors and calm Clydesdales, which would later steal the show by pulling Gussie Busch in to the stadium on a beer wagon. Rabid fans were already streaming from the parking lots chanting, waving pennants, buzzing in anticipation of a Redbird comeback against the Brewers, who led the Series three games to two. Although tickets were hard to find, I had been able to get them for two of the home playoff games with the Atlanta Braves as well as both of the Series games already played in St. Louis. But now things looked bleak.

"Well," I said halfheartedly, not very hopeful about my last shot. "I met George Hendrick the other night."

"Hendrick," Kenny snapped, "you mean *the* George Hendrick, the Cardinal rightfielder?"

My one brief meeting with Silent George had occurred in a rather unusual way. On the night of the first National League playoff game in St. Louis against the Braves, I was working at the local Playboy Club as a stand-up comedian. The crowd was sparse, and like everyone else in St. Louis, the members of my audience seemed to be pooped from the long day of rain and game delays and, finally, cancellation. But, despite the lack of enthusiasm in the nightclub, Hendrick and his two companions apparently enjoyed the show, and later they invited me to join them at their table. We talked about baseball and comedy and laughed about the horrors of performing either athletically or comically in front of hostile crowds.

"I thought he wouldn't talk to the press," Kenny said.

"I'm not the press, I'm a fan," I replied. "And he said if I got to a Series game to give him a call in the locker room, and he'd have me down to meet some of the guys."

"Will he have extra tickets?"

"I doubt it."

The stage was set. At exactly 5:11 p.m. we entered the Cardinal office on the street level at Busch Stadium. Determined to appear confident, I walked briskly toward the World Series temporary reception desk and immediately encountered the home-run king Roger Maris and sportscaster Joe Garagiola. Pausing very briefly to catch my breath, I moved through the crowded room. Because I'd urged Kenny and the boys to drive the 500 miles and because I was the guy who hadn't been able to find a single ticket in spite of a day of frantic phone calling, I was willing to try anything. I brushed past the home-run king and calmly said to the receptionist. "Call George and tell him Grady Jim is here."

The woman looked up from the desk without expression, a veteran at repulsing gate-crashers and con artists. She examined my face, apparently trying to determine if I were telling the truth. "What's your name?" she said sharply.

"Grady Jim," I repeated with a devil-may-care tone. "Call George Hendrick, please, he's looking for us downstairs."

When in doubt, be bold. Act like you know what you are doing, right? That's what we always say.

With a weary sigh, the woman picked up the phone and dialed. Dozens of busy journalists, ballplayers' friends, Anheuser-Busch big shots and other notables milled about the room waiting to be escorted inside the stadium to do whatever it is people do who are lucky enough to get into the inner sanctum.

"Hello, is George in the locker room?" the receptionist asked.

There was a pause; it seemed a very long time while she awaited word. Was he on the field already? Would he remember our brief conversation? How many other calls just like this one had he received today?

Finally she said, "Hello, George, there's a Grady Jim here to see you, and he's got some kids with him."

Perspiration popped out along my upper lip and a cold chill crawled up my rigid spine. The woman repeated my name, and I knew George had said, "Who?"

"Grady Jim. He says you're looking for him."

Another silence. Then she hung up the phone and looked at me, again without expression. I imagined her saying, "You jerk! Clear out!" Instead she said, "OK, sign the clipboard and follow the usher over there."

Like something out of *Alice's Adventures in Wonderland*, the locked door clicked and opened wide. We hurried through it behind the usher. Dignitaries and club officials rushing about with clipboards and shouting orders to gofers ignored us as we made our way to the stairs leading downward to the Cardinal locker room. Kenny mumbled in my ear, "I can't believe this!"

"Neither can I," I said. "Stay close and keep the boys near you." Through a hallway we hustled, but our usher escort disappeared in the tangle of humanity. At the bottom of the stairs we turned left. I looked for the familiar face of Silent George. Sure enough, there he was, with a huge smile, buttoning his famous long-legged, double-knit pants.

"Hi, fellas," he said softly. "Stick close and we'll walk out to the dugout, and after batting practice, we'll come back to the locker room and chat awhile."

From that point, the details melt together like a technicolor dream. Passing Tom Seaver and Tony Kubek in the tunnel, we walked with Hendrick to the dugout and looked out at the Astroturf field. Was that Whitey Herzog? Who was that NBC guy? Hundreds of media people. Crack of bat on ball. Cameras clicking. Busch Stadium empty like a vast cavern reaching upward. And, above, the ubiquitous Goodyear Blimp, now benevolently droning into the wind.

Only 12 brief hours after leaving their warm beds in Oklahoma, Little Leaguers Jason and Jared sat in the dugout of the St. Louis Cardinals. Tommy Herr walked by. Ozzie Smith sat only a few feet away. Ted Simmons, Dick Enberg, Bob Costas, Jack Buck showed up. Then it was back to the locker room with Hendrick. Players, coaches, and visitors walked in and out of the busy clubhouse, some chatting with reporters, others sitting on stools in front of their lockers patiently awaiting one of the most important events of their lives. Jim Kaat, 43 years old and in his 24th season, stood only a few feet away talking quietly with John Stuper, the 25-year-old starting pitcher. A small sandbox cum spittoon sat in the middle of the floor; it seemed out of place until I remembered that modern ball players are still men of great expectorations.

Hendrick sat the two boys down on his locker stool and wiped the perspiration from his face. Keith Hernandez walked hurriedly to the adjoining locker and asked George for a pen so that he could autograph some pictures. "Keith, meet Jason and Jared from Oklahoma," said Hendrick.

Hernandez smiled, shook hands with the speechless boys and their daddy. Hendrick, with the game only an hour or so away, sat down and pulled two bright red World Series duffel bags from his locker. The bags were filled with all kinds of souvenirs that would go back to Oklahoma and be pawed over by the boys' school friends. A new baseball was casually tossed into each bag, which held note pads with Cardinal emblems, wristbands and batting gloves. Then, without a word, the Silent One walked into the equipment room and reappeared carrying two Louisville Sluggers, George Hendrick-autographed bats. They were the real thing. The number 25 — Hendrick's — was nearly inscribed on the knobs, and three single strips of tape about one inch apart were wrapped around the handles. The bats were ready for World Series action. "Here you go, fellas, something to take home from the Series," said Hendrick. The boys were stunned. Kenny smiled and muttered many thank-yous.

After handshakes all around, the delirious four left the confines of the future world champions' locker room...still without tickets. I didn't have the heart to ask Hendrick for player passes, although I was sorely tempted. I felt that he had done enough. I said, "Hit a home run for us, George."

"I won't hit one if they keep pitching me low and outside," he said matter-of-factly. "I'll have to keep hitting them up the middle." The Brewers did continue to throw low and outside. Hendrick slapped two singles, one to left centerfield and one to right, in Game 6 and knocked in the winning run in Game 7 on a sharp single to right center.

Lugging duffel bags and bats and an autographed newspaper article on Hendrick, we made our way up the stairs. My mind raced. We could turn right at the main corridor and walk out the stadium door. I knew it was likely we would not find our way back in for the game. Because we had no tickets. That would be the honest thing to do. Or we could turn left and illegally enter the area behind the box seats. Though we would not have a place to sit, we'd be inside the stadium and could watch the game in the standing-room-only area.

What should be done in front of the impressionable youngsters? Well, there is a time to be honorable and to do what is right in the eyes of the law. But there is also a time to get into the World Series any way you can.

I jerked Kenny by the arm and he grabbed Jason, who nabbed Jared, and we hustled through the double doors in to the box-seat area. During Game 6 of the 1982 Series, a bedraggled group of four, carrying duffel bags filled with World Series souvenirs and two George Hendrick Model Louisville Sluggers, wandered from section to section, avoiding ushers and ticket-checkers.

Each time Hendrick was at bat, five times in all, there came, from a different location in the stadium, an extra chorus of wildly enthusiastic screaming — first from behind home plate, later, in the third inning, from somewhere down the leftfield line, and still later, in the seventh, from just above the Stadium Club.

One Leg at a Time

"I hope we don't get the Gooden Machine tonight," said a meek voice from the back seat of the car as I drove my nine-year-old son and two teammates to their baseball game. "Me too!" said another. "It throws too fast and the ball makes me nervous."

I had to smile. The boys were about to face an electrical pitching machine at Marshall Field in Kirkwood, Mo., one that fired fastballs right down the middle of the plate at a hittable 55 miles per hour. However, acting as pitcher for both teams, the machine had struck out 34 batters in seven innings the previous week and had been immediately dubbed the Gooden Machine, after Mets pitcher Dwight Gooden. (We later learned that the machine was not properly adjusted and was firing the ball at about 65 mph.)

"Dad, do you think we'll get the Gooden Machine?"

"I don't know, boys. But you can hit it. Think positive!" I said, offering typical paternal encouragement against insurmountable odds.

As I spoke, my mind drifted back 30 years to a similar conversation about another pitching machine, not an electrical one, but a living, breathing hard-throwing legend from Barling, Ark., named Tommy (Fishhook) Smith.

"Just remember boys, he puts his pants on just like you do ...one leg at a time," my father said from the driver's seat of our 1954 Pontiac.

"Yeah, Dad, but just look at the legs he's putting in those pants!" I said.

Laughter erupted from the back seat where my brother, David, Joe Stafford and Tommy Shockley nervously pounded their fists into old ball gloves.

Our annual trip to play in the Boys' Club tournament at Lion's Park in Fort Smith was the highlight of the summer. Compared to our rocky, dandelion-infested field behind the Greenwood Elementary School, Lion's Park seemed like a miniature replica of a major league ballpark. It had an outfield fence, real dugouts, stands for our parents, plus a manicured grass infield with a real pitcher's mound.

However, our joy on that particular evening was tempered by the knowledge that Tommy (Fishhook) Smith would be on that mound. He was big for his age — a hulking 160 pounds — and he had picked up his nickname not for his intimate knowledge of fishing but rather for his wicked, downward breaking curveball.

To make matters worse, Fishhook's older brother, Hal, was a catcher for the St. Louis Cardinals, and it was agreed that no mortal could hit the brother of an actual major league catcher. Joe was distantly related to Fishhook, which is to say a solid second cousin by marriage, and he had, the year before, hit a Tommy Smith fastball. No small task. But now Tommy had added a curve, and *nobody*, not even a second cousin, could touch the hook.

Assuming you were a righthanded batter, the ball started right at your head, a spinning, sizzling, whirring horsehide. The batter's left foot instinctively lurched toward the third base dugout as if an invisible wire were tied to the ankle.

Some kids — mercy forbids naming names — completely panicked at the sight of Fishhook's approaching curveball and immediately hit the deck, only to hear the umpire say, almost apologetically, "Uh, strike three, son."

My father, understanding our anxieties, tried to offer hope and coaching. But how could he truly understand? He had been a great hitter in his day. According to legend, on July 4, 1925, he had hit four shots "out in the pecan trees" off a 15-year-old from Lucas, Ark., named Jerome Dean — Dizzy they called him when he won 30 games for the Cardinals in 1934.

And, in 1943, Dad faced Warren Spahn, who won 367 games before he retired in 1965. He was pitching for Fort Chaffee during his three-year hitch in the Army. One Sunday afternoon Fort Chaffee's team drove over and played a Greenwood town team behind the county courthouse. My dad was the Greenwood first baseman. He never said if he got a hit off Spahn or not, but we assumed he did.

Since my father was the high school basketball and football coach, he was accustomed to giving pregame pep talks. "You can do it," he urged, "if you think you can. You've got to believe in yourself!"

We tried valiantly, but Tommy believed in himself, too, and blew us away, something like 16-0. Our assumption was correct: A mere mortal can't hit the brother of a major league catcher.

That was 30 years ago.

We're all grown now. My brother, David, became an all-conference pitcher at Arkansas Tech in 1966 and '67. Joe was the starting catcher for the Arkansas Razorbacks from 1965 to '67. Tommy Shockley went to Vietnam and now works for Merle Haggard.

And Tommy Smith? He signed a pro contract with the St. Louis Cardinals in 1964 and was a first baseman for the

Double A Arkansas Travelers. He never made it as far as his brother, Hal, though.

Just then, the conversation behind me brought me back to the present. "If we have to face the Gooden Machine we'll all strike out," said a voice.

"I couldn't see the ball last time," said another. "I just heard it hit the umpire."

When the third kid said, "I think I'll join the band," I had heard enough.

As we stopped at a red light, I turned and practically yelled, "Now listen, guys, you can hit that machine! Just remember, he puts his pants on just like you do.... Oh, never mind."

They were giggling so much I don't think they heard me mumble, "Just be thankful the dang thing can't throw a curveball."

Walking with Ghosts in Ione

A cold drizzle had begun to fall as I turned off Highway 23 into the old school yard in tiny (pop. 57 and declining) community of Ione, Ark., and gazed for the first time at the weed-covered baseball field. Through the sheet of gray mist I saw them — the ghosts I had expected to see and therefore did see. Wet weeds crunched under my feet as I walked slowly to where the shortstop would have played.

I was elated that the field was still there. Before my visit, Lorena Wooten Bush had assured me that it was remarkably well preserved, almost exactly as it had been in 1910, when she lived across the street and her cousin Aaron Ward played there. I had feared that the field would be different. After all, nearly 80 years, more than a dozen presidents, two world wars, and radio and television had changed the world considerably. Surely someone had put up a feedlot in the infield or a gas station along the third base line.

But no, there it was as plain as day. Plain as 1910. Apparently this little community had given up the economic struggle, died a quiet death, and left the old school house and the ball field preserved, suspended in time exactly as it was in its heyday.

I got out of my rental car and walked through the stand of trees that lined the first base side of the field, trees that had provided shade on hot summer days for the hundreds of spectators who came out to cheer for their town teams. I could almost see the vendors hawking their wares: lemonade, sodie-waters out of tubs and, according to Hill Turner, who played here in the '20s and still lives just a Ruthian shot behind right field, ice cream.

The field remains so flat that, if you were to give the grass a good mowing, set up some bases and add a wire backstop, you might get farm boys from Lucas, Washburn, Barber, and Milltown to come out of the hills for one more tournament. As they did long ago, they would stay in the homes of townspeople.

I looked down into the grass as I neared the shortstop area and kicked the dirt. It occurred to me that grass changes and that trees grow but that dirt — this loamy, pebble-filled soil — stays the same. So I kicked down through the grass, scuffing at the very earth on which Aaron Ward had stood. "Right here, this is it," I said to no one in particular. I had to laugh at myself, standing in a soft rain in the middle of a flat field in a tiny town in the hills of Arkansas reconstructing moments in the life of a ballplayer whose career had come to fascinate me, although I can't explain exactly why, beyond some common geographic roots.

My eyes scoured every square foot of the infield. I thought about my father, who had played on this same field in the '20s and '30s. He wanted to be a major leaguer, and according to eyewitnesses he was "one of the best." Instead, he decided to go to college and become a high school teacher and coach. Which he did, settling in nearby Greenwood, where he lived for 40 years.

My thoughts turned back to Aaron, as I had begun to call him. After having listened to Lorena Bush talk about her childhood playmate and first cousin, I felt I knew him. The son of Tom and Molly Ward of Booneville, Aaron joined the New York Yankees as an infielder in 1917 and became their starting second baseman in 1921. He played in three World Series, hitting two home runs in the '22 Series and batting .417 in the '23 Series. While he performed his heroics, back in Arkansas, Tom and Molly stood with several hundred people outside the telegraph office in Fort Smith getting inning-by-inning accounts of the games.

Following the '23 Series, Aaron returned to Ione driving a new Marmon convertible. His wife, Inez, who was wearing a stunning red dress, was seated beside him. "Yes sir, I remember that day," Harold Scharbor said while sitting on his front porch shortly before his death earlier this year. "Yeah, Aaron Ward drove through here, right down that highway, right there in a big convertible, and his wife was with him. It was the first convertible car I'd ever seen, and it was the first time I'd ever seen a woman in a red dress."

I looked up at the sky. The drizzle had intensified to a gray December shower, but I wasn't ready to go. Feeling for the tape recorder in my coat pocket. I walked to the mound, or within a few feet of where it certainly must have been, assuming home plate had been just this side of the pole, as I had been told. I pulled the tape recorder out of my pocket and punched the "play" button. I felt the rain and heard Lorena's soft, clear voice:

"They'd play three or four days in a row — tournaments," she said. "Teams would come from all over because that field was the best one in the area. Back then the town had stores, shops, two blacksmiths, a doctor. I lived in cousin Aaron's home for awhile. He and his daddy, Tom, were ball crazy.

"But Aaron wasn't the only one who became a famous ballplayer from this area. Two other little boys ran around out there, lived right next door, actually. They came over and picked cotton for my daddy. They were my age, and when they were five, six, and seven, they watched Aaron play ball. Their daddy's name was Albert Dean; their mama was a Nelson. The Nelsons were the best ballplayers in the area. Albert was the umpire on many occasions.

"One day they were having a big game. A crowd of people had come, and they were watching Aaron because he'd become known as something special and he was. Anyway, Albert was umpiring, and the sheriff shows up and walks right out to the pitcher's mound. Albert would stand behind the pitcher when he umpired, see. Well, the sheriff walks right up and puts handcuffs on Albert Dean and takes him away. Later I asked my daddy, 'Daddy, why did they take Mr. Dean away?' He said, 'Well, hon, they said he was operating a blind pig.'

"I thought, What in the world were they operating on a blind pig for? Of course, he was operating a still. They called it a blind pig. Those two little boys grew up to be just like my cousin Aaron. They became major league ballplayers."

I turned off the recorder. Those two Dean boys, Jay and Paul, did very well for themselves as Dizzy and Daffy Dean of the St. Louis Cardinals' Gashouse Gang. I'd heard about them all my life. Jay Hanna Dean was a feared pitcher and like most of the other boys played barefoot. According to the late Bill Woody who often played against the Dean boys, "We would put rocks on the mound when Diz was going to pitch. About the third inning we'd start yelling at him, 'Hey, Jay, how's them feet feeling'?' He never let on like it bothered him."

"After the Yankees won the Series in '23," said Lorena, "Aaron pretty much became a hero around here. His picture was in the Fort Smith paper with the check for $6,000, which was his winner's share. That was so much money in those days, more than his yearly salary. We were all so excited and proud. Later that fall, Aaron went moose hunting in Canada with Babe Ruth, Waite Hoyt and a man named Bob Meusel. People used to get him mixed up with Stan Musial years later — I mean in talk around town here — but it was Bob Meusel. Anyway, after the hunt, Babe Ruth, Waite Hoyt and Bob Meusel came back to Fort Smith on the train. Tom and Molly moved out of their house — they were living in Fort Smith at that time — and let them all stay there. They'd play golf every day out at the old Fort Smith Country Club, and at night they'd have a big dinner and party and dance. I was Waite Hoyt's date. Yes sir, I went with Waite Hoyt. We had fun. Aaron was a good-looking, witty young man. The girls just loved him.

"Well — and I do hate to have to mention the sad part — but Aaron began to drink during those years. He had always been the best at everything. He could hunt, fish, run, jump, do anything. He could stand up in the saddle on the back of a horse while it was running full speed, and he often did it for a show. And he was the best dancer around, even though his mother, Molly, was a very, very strict Baptist and wouldn't allow him to go with girls or to the dances. He would slip out of his room at night and go to the dances.

"Anyway, he started drinking with the celebrities of New York because he was such a personable boy. We heard all kinds of stories. It like to killed his mother. Inez left Aaron in 1927, with their two daughters. She still loved him, though. A few years later, after Aaron was out of baseball, he was driving through Morrilton, and he stopped and visited Inez. She had remarried. He found her in the barn churning butter and laughed. She had been a real looker and had enjoyed the social whirl. But she laughed, too. He said, 'I didn't think I'd ever see you churning butter.' She said, 'Well, I probably never would have if I'd stayed with you.' We always felt they loved each other, but she couldn't stand his drinking. It's a sad ending I'm afraid. Aaron lost businesses, tried to hold baseball jobs, worked in the Oklahoma oil fields. He even managed a ball club in Little Rock one year but lost the job. It was sad. He died in New Orleans in 1961."

I turned off the recorder and walked back to the car. The rain stopped, and I paused for a last look at the field. Suddenly, I could see all the way back to 1910 and Aaron Ward at shortstop, a young man with such talent that, of all the kids playing on all the ball fields all over the country, he would be the one to play second for the Yankees. He would be the one designated by Babe Ruth as his favorite second baseman. He would be the guy who would face Ty Cobb's sharpened spikes, catch Tris Speaker's line drives. And he would be the second baseman who played on the day Yankee Stadium was opened.

In a flash, too, I saw 1926 and the Dean boys: Dizzy, just 15 years old, wearing coveralls, barefoot, grinning and saying, "Here she comes!" as he fired that sizzling fastball to his older brother, Elmer; and little brother Paul at shortstop. I saw my father, Grady, too, and his brothers over from Milltown to challenge the Dean boys. The whole scene was clear: trees, shade, wagons, tethered horses, a rare auto sputtering down the dirt road — all in this thriving community, hidden in the quiet hills. But that was long ago.

I put the car in gear and drove on to Little Rock, around the bend and a world away.

PART III
Adults Only

Queen Bee

My secretary, Jane Seagraves, was walking out the door for a luncheon date with Dr. Kathy Cramer, the well known St. Louis psychologist. I was shooting hoops with a whiffle ball and thinking about a round of afternoon golf.

"Where are you meeting the beautiful doctor for lunch?" I asked in a casual manner.

"Schniedhorsts. See you later," she said.

I had met Dr. Cramer six years earlier in 1982 and had since that time seen her being interviewed on various TV news shows. Her shockingly beautiful blue eyes, blonde hair, and hour-glass figure were impossible to forget.

"Well," I said, recalling the gorgeous blue eyes, the big smile and the unforgettable breasts, "perhaps I should go along and maybe be of some assistance?"

"Grady, you hate business lunches."

"Is Dr. Cramer single?"

"Yes, I believe so."

Single myself, I felt it my duty to meet and dialogue with as many single women as possible and learn perchance the secrets of a modern relationship. And besides, Dr. Cramer was a psychologist of some renown and probably knew all about the whole women-are-from-Venus-and-men-are-from-some-other-far-off-lost-planet thing. After Jane left, I drove directly to the restaurant.

I was seated on a bar stool watching the restaurant door. I waited. And waited. Twenty minutes later than planned, a trait that would become familiar to me and perhaps should have served as a warning signal, she walked through the door.

Any warning signals that may or may not have been obvious at the time went unheeded. For when she entered a room, she entered a room. My head reeled, my heart pumped, and I heard myself writing a Mickey Spillane novel: "When she walked into that joint with that cloud-burst of blonde curls falling upon her shoulders you could hear heads turning as far away as Peoria and when she nonchalantly strode across that room in that $600 St. John's suit adorning as it was the very quintessence of womanhood physically and intellectually, and when she looked me in the eye and I saw those baby blues, my hand went limp in hers and my jaw hung open for just an instant too long. I mumbled something and knew immediately it was love at first sight."

I was totally enamored.

Her smile lit up the dark decor of the restaurant and I wasn't the only guy in the room who couldn't take his eyes off her. As we talked about brochures, agents, demo tapes and the use of humor in keynote speaking I stole glances and studied her. She was intelligent, quick to laugh, inquisitive, a good listener and brilliant conversationalist. I had never met a more impressive woman. Her beauty brightened the room and the very slight scar over the left side of her upper lip only served to make her even more mysterious and intriguing. I was single, 41 years old when suddenly, out of the blue, this blonde Ph.D. walks into my life and Wham Bam Thank You, Ma'am.

We went to lunch a few days later and became instant friends. Kathy is easy to like. What's not to like? We became friends and although we did not become romantically involved we went to dinners, parties, movies and once traveled together to San Antonio, Texas where she saw me perform for the first time.

In a few months I was totally smitten. Kathy Cramer was my only desire, goal and consuming passion. It seemed to me it would be perfect but from her perspective it was not. She was unsure about me and my intentions.

One night I called to see if she was free to go out for a casual dinner and discovered another man at her house. They were going to the symphony for a formal evening.

It was the loneliest night of my life. I paced back and forth in my Kirkwood apartment insanely jealous, bitterly disappointed and cloaked in a cloud of depression.

As the long night wore on I began to assess the situation:

What did I have to offer Kathy Cramer, the beautiful Ph.D., born and educated in the finest schools, a "Villa Girl" (as I would discover much later they were called). She was life-long friends with many of the city's wealthiest daughters (for example, the great grandniece of old J.C. Penney himself); or the granddaughter of the man who owned the St. Louis Browns; and even more impressive to me, she had attended school with the daughter of none other than Stan The Man Musial.

Grady Jim Robinson, from Greenwood, Arkansas, the second son of a football coach, stand-up comic, a writer, a storyteller, a mystic.

I paced the floor racking my brain for a plan that might counter a formal night at the symphony listening to all those Bachs, Beethovens, and Brahms. I sipped scotch and cried and paced and looked into the face of my mother whose picture hung on he wall. And there was a picture of my father and my older brother and little me, the second son, the surprise they said who came into their life a year or two before they had intended.

Then it hit me. Mom often told the story of daddy taking her on special picnics along the banks of small stream near Greenwood. He would surprise her with sandwiches, corn on the cob and home grown tomatoes. That's it.

Within days I had made plans to take Kathy to lunch. I prepared a picnic basket with fried chicken, corn on the cob, cole slaw, grapes and a bottle of good wine. I wore my tuxedo, rented a limousine, wrote a special song, brought along a book of poems and my guitar.

I arrived at her office and knocked on the door. She came to the door.

"Grady Jim Robinson, what in the world is going on?"

"We're going to lunch, a picnic lunch." I announced.

As she settled into the back seat of the limo she looked at me suspiciously and asked, "Why are you doing this?"

There was only one reason I could think of and luckily it came out in the right way. I said simply, "Because you deserve it."

She began to cry. Then she looked at me in a very pleasant way.

I held her hand as we rode to my appointed picnic spot. I spread the blanket and got out the wine and chicken and fruit. We ate the chicken and drank the wine. I read to her a poem I had chosen by E.B. White called "The Flight of the Queen Bee." It tells of the queen bee who flies higher and higher as her pursuers attempt to keep up. She flies higher and higher as her many pursuers drop out one by one until there is only one strong stud bee left. He is triumphant. She chooses to mate with him. And then, unfortunately, he dies a slow, agonizing death in the very act of mating. Of course, I ignored that part.

Grady Jim and Kathy during happy times. A night on the town in Monte Carlo.

Then I pulled out the guitar and sang a song I had written for the occasion called, "Here Comes That R Word Again."

I met a pretty woman in a seminar,
a woman with a Ph.D.
Big blue eyes, my, what a surprise
a Doctor of Psychology.

We went to lunch and I had a hunch
That she sorta, kinda liked me,
So I shot from the hip
and kissed her on the lips...
don't try it with a Ph.D.

No shootin' from the hip
No kissin' on the lip
til' you hammer out a relationship.
Kissin's not a sin, but relatin' is in
HERE COMES THAT "R" WORD AGAIN.

As I sang the song Kathy smiled and looked at me with newfound interest. She seemed to be looking through me, trying to see what was inside, trying to see the future. She knew I was serious about her. She was getting the message.

Not to be outdone by any other stud bee who might attempt to fly higher I reached into my pocket and pulled out two first class tickets to Hawaii.

"Kathy, would you like to go to Hawaii with me for one week?"

"Grady!"

The Queen Bee couldn't fly much higher and I was buzzing closer and closer.

Kathy Cramer looked at me with *that* look in her blue eyes, a look I would learn to enjoy. She looked at my mouth and my forehead and my hair and then into my eyes. I could feel her looking me over very carefully. It had to be love. What else could it be?

"I'll think about the trip," she said softly and kissed me.

"I've got to go to the airport," I said suddenly. "Wow, the time has gotten away from us. I'm flying to Wichita this afternoon for a speech tonight. I'll have to go in my tux."

"Did you bring the ticket?"

"Yes, thank God."

We drove to the airport. As we pulled up to the front door I prepared to jump out of the limo and run for gate 45.

"Wait!" She said.

"Kathy, this is going to be close. I gotta hustle."

"Wait a second," she said. Laughing and bounding with energy in a style that I would learn to appreciate, she jumped from the limo and announced, "I'm going with you!" I loved such outrageous spontaneity, and admired her even more. I was elated. I had won her. The queen was choosing me.

Kathy jumped out of the limo and hurried to the TWA counter, whipped out her American Express card and purchased a first-class round-trip ticket to Wichita. We held hands all the way and talked about Carl Jung, Pierre Teilhard de Chardin, Joseph Campbell, literature, art and baseball.

Upon landing she taxied to a local mall, bought a beautiful dress and hurried back for the cocktail hour at the convention.

I did my speech in the tux, and that night in a suite overlooking the Arkansas River in the old Mulebach Hotel we became One. The Queen Bee had chosen.

And that was the beginning of my slow, agonizing, downward spiral of death.

Married November 26, 1988. Honeymoon in Vail and Aspen. February to New Orleans for NSA where I do "Class Clown: The Inward Journey."

My world suddenly shifts into a different zone. New York, The Pierre, Phantom of the Opera, Cats, La Bernadin, a Rolex, Smith and Wollensky, The Village, SOHO where she tries on outfits and looks so stunning that pedestrian traffic is stopped on the sidewalk outside the shop. Carmel, San Francisco and the Million Dollar Round Table, in no particular order over the next few years.

Bermuda for snorkeling, Kathy in her tiny bikini creating a sensation on the boat dock and me fighting off pirates. Key Largo where we drive for a long time and she is urging me to stop and ask directions and I say there will be a sign somewhere and we end up half way to Key West. I don't think she ever got over that one.

Our life may be best understood in light of the week long trip to Paris. On New Year's Eve we flew TWA first class to Paris. At 3 a.m. we walked the Champs Élysées and found pizza with eggs on top and wine, walked for miles toward the West Bank found Chartres the Mona Lisa, Venus DeMilo, Michelangelo, Leonardo Da Vinci and experienced the aesthetic arrest of a lifetime. On to Shakespeare and Co., where I introduced myself to the ghosts of James Joyce, Samuel Beckett, T.S. Eliot, Ezra Pound, Ernest Hemingway, and Sylvia Beach.

She decided we'd fly up to Monte Carlo for the weekend where we gambled and ate fabulous food then returned to Paris for the flight home.

Harbor Springs to hobnob with the very rich. Chicago to the Jungian Institute to explore the role of the Shekinah in Jewish Myth; San Fran for Systems Thinking with Scott Peck, Fritjof Capra and Meg Wheatley; New Hampshire for the Joseph Campbell Festival with Mathew Fox, Thomas Moore, Jean Shinoda Bolen, books, books, books.

Then the cabin at Innsbrook, weekends on the little lake, bass boat and fishing, parties and drinking on the pontoon boat.

Ryan off to Boston College. We drive to Provincetown, Cape Cod for a brief holiday but she doesn't like the accommodations and we move on to Nantucket where she insists we stay in dock side cabins for $450 per day and for the first time I feel something very wrong in our life.

It was during that trip that I realized that she had not looked at me in that special way in a long, long time.

Another Thanksgiving Day Run

I paced nervously on Argonne Avenue as I mentally prepared for the ordeal ahead. The moment had come. All the dreaming, all the training was over. The Thanksgiving Three-Mile Run from the Kirkwood train station to Webster Groves is the race I prepare for each year. I carefully plan my workout schedule so that my body will be at its physical peak by Thanksgiving morning.

I looked over my competition: a ragtag group of accountants, balding lawyers, housewives and retirees, all dressed in a varied assortment of colorful running suits, shoes and tights.

Some — obviously the more inexperienced runners — stripped to shorts and T-shirts in the freezing temperatures. Not me. Any experienced runner knows you must keep the body warm, so I wore two pairs of socks, thermal underwear, sweatpants, two sweatshirts, a windbreaker, leather gloves (keep those extremities warm) and a stocking cap.

We gathered in front of the Kirkwood train station. It was almost time.

I was ready.

Some eager beavers warmed up by running around the block, expending precious energy. Fools! I warmed up by wearing plenty of clothes. Younger runners often make that fatal mistake. They warm up; I conserve energy, protein and fat. And when the race begins I start slowly, build in the middle and...Zoom!

The starter finally said, "Go!" and 3,000 runners of various sizes, shapes and running experience attempted to run west on Argonne, all in one spot, a mass of humanity, each of us eager to reach down deep and find our true stuff.

Every fiber of my perfectly trained body cried out for instant speed, but, being a runner of experience and realizing I hadn't actually worked out since September, I held back.

We jockeyed for position, settled into a pace and found our level of competition within the pack. Then, we passed Jeremiah's Restaurant made the U-turn and wobbled back down the other side of Argonne. OK, the pace was slow. But, it was early!

After almost 300 yards I was pumping sweat like a hook and ladder truck and wisely shed the windbreaker. I immediately felt stronger and smiled at the mass of women and children trudging pitifully in front of me. I would pass them like a picket fence.

We runners face psychological barriers during the long, lonely ordeal of a race, and at each barrier there is a decision to be made: Will I stop and give in to the pain? Or, will I go on and conquer? Each positive choice makes you tougher, stronger and purer in spirit; this is where we runners contact the true inner self.

On Adams, as we settled into our pace, I encountered the first inner voice, along with a splitting pain in my side. The voice said, "Hey, you old goat, you haven't run in months! Drop out or die!"

Sure, I was tempted. Better men than I have succumbed. I almost did. But, then I thought of all the people who believed in me, the hours of training at Jeremiah's, the embarrassment of dropping out first.... I went on.

At Sappington, realizing the pack was edging ahead, that even the women and children were fading in the distance, I discarded two more sweatshirts, the leather gloves and the stocking cap. Immediately I felt fresher, called on all of my inner resources and maintained the same pace. But, again, that inner voice, that dreaded demon of doubt, said, "You idiot! You haven't gone a mile yet, and you're already about to croak. Drop out, Lard Thighs!"

I admit it. I thought about it. I glanced to my right where suddenly three ladies passed me chatting busily about turkey and dressing, Christmas shopping and diets, running seemingly without struggle. I looked behind me to make sure no runners were gaining on me. There were no runners gaining on me, because there were no runners behind me — none!

At the mile mark a clock person shouted, "...9:43, 9:44, 9:45!" as we sped by. The inner voice said, "Hey, I don't think you're going to win this year." I didn't listen. I knew there was still a chance. As long as there is a chance, just a smidge of a chance to win the gold, finish first, become champion, a man must go on.

My running form was suffering somewhat at the two-mile mark. It was a grisly sight. Toes pointed outward, legs wobble noticeably, and the mouth tends to hang open while emitting loud gasps.

Then, I saw him. A skinny kid in a St. Louis Running Club T-shirt was running directly toward me. He had run the entire route, three miles to Webster Groves, turned at the train station and was running back to Kirkwood. He was blazing along in comfortable fashion, and then, I knew. It was not going to be my year.

I immediately stopped running and collapsed into the nearest yard.

Hey, who needs second place, right?

A Day at the Races

Turning 50 and getting the divorce in the same year wasn't so bad. But it irritated me when the shrink said I seemed to have some "problem with my masculinity."

"What do you mean?" I snapped in defense. "Don't I fish and play golf and watch football?"

"Grady, your recent dreams tell me you have a problem with male competition. Maybe that's why things have, you know, become difficult. You have some aversion to masculine competition."

"Now wait just a minute. I've been competing all my life."

"You've admitted yourself that you have depended too much on your artistic, connecting, feeling side in your life. You've been a minister, comedian, storyteller, all artistic vocations. Don't you see?"

I had to think about that. A problem with male competition. Maybe that's why I made the trip back to Arkansas to visit my brother, catch some bass, shoot a deer or two, change some oil, smoke cigars, interact with the opposite sex and go to the horse races. An aversion to head-on competition with males, indeed!

After a perfect race day morning at the famed old Arlington Hotel in Hot Springs, which includes a southern — I might add a very masculine — breakfast of steak and eggs, a pile of grits, fried potatoes, biscuits and gravy, coffee and a Budweiser, I spent time on the veranda smoking a cigar, spitting and scratching and carefully studying the racing form.

I arrived at Oaklawn Park early and pulled into the first parking spot at Booger T's Bar and Grub and prepared to absorb the sights and sounds, the hustle and bustle of race day. Wearing my cowboy boots, jeans, denim shirt and a fine sports coat which announced to all available southern belles that this is a real horse player, I looked for a suitable bar stool where I continued to study the racing form, await the arrival of hordes of southern women and contemplate the meaning of head-on competition.

I was on my second Bloody Mary when an old man walked in.

Finally, I thought, a horseplayer. Now we can have some manly horse talk, hot tips, gaming and gambling talk. He wore a cap with a farm equipment company logo on top. He was a bit bleary eyed I assumed from excessive partying after the big race of the previous day but seemed anxious to start the new day of racing and high living that we horse men enjoy.

"So," I said casually, not wanting to appear like a novice, "who you like today?"

He glanced at the bartender and then almost whispered, "BuddyGottaDime!" For me, being into poetry, words, my artistic side and all, the names of the horses are part of what makes horseracing fun. On my racing form I had already spotted some all time favorite names that brought a smile:

"Shoutcalpurina," "Twila ChooChoo," and "Ride With Pancho." I didn't immediately recognize his favorite, "BuddyGottaDime," but I would remember that tip for sure.

"Which race is he in?" I whispered.

He refused to divulge further information.

I paid up and strode out into the drizzling rain where racing fans were now arriving for the day of racing.

I've learned over the years — actually I've only been to the races one other time — but having a sixth sense about horse flesh I know it's all about speed and heart. Down that home stretch fighting with the descendants of Ali Sheba and Secretariat. Compete or die. There's that word again. Competition, is that it? Is that life? Head-to-head competition and if you have a problem with that you're probably a natural born loser. If you can't make the grade, sit in the shade.

I'm standing at the rail watching the field approach the gate. The horses are beautiful.

I've got $10 on *Mover* to *Show*, $10 to win on *J.J. Ray*.

I'm all set. "They're in the gate," the track announcer says. After the day at the races I'll take my winnings and drive over to Sheridan to see my brother and his family. Big Dave has lived an exemplary life. He's been a solid citizen, family man, a Rotarian, and church leader. He has competed well. Even when we were kids Dave was a top competitor in sports, grades, leadership in school and church. I wanted to be like him. I wanted to compete well, to be successful, to be happy with myself.

They're off.

The horses explode from the gate and the most important part of the race quickly unfolds as they literally jockey for position thundering toward the first turn, dirt clods flying, crowd roaring. My God, it's in my blood!

JJ Ray is four lengths out front just as I predicted. They roar around the first turn, fly down the backstretch barely visible through the trees so I hurry to the grandstands for a better view.

Now it's getting serious and people start yelling. Around the second turn they come and excitement fills the air as the most exciting part of the race unfolds...the home stretch where the will to win, heart and heritage, a million years of evolution is made manifest in the flesh.

"AND DOWN THE STRETCH THEY COME...." shouts the track announcer. It's payoff time. Who's got the guts, the will to win?

I've got money on JJ Ray, Mover, Take Affirm Hold and Knobgobbler.

And down the stretch comes the winner — Big Fuzzy.

Who?

Oh, well. Can't win 'em all. I smile knowingly at all the poor slobs that scream in anguish, tear up tickets and angrily throw them down, curse the sky and the racing gods and all other gods, and storm to the concession stand to drowned their disappointments in beer. I casually stroll inside, purchase some old scotch, light a cigar and scan the racing form for the next race. I know horses. I'll pick plenty of winners. No hurry. I walk by the paddock where I carefully study the horse I am interested in. I read The Horse Whisperer long before Robert Redford. I know horseflesh. I study every muscle, every move and line and look deep into their eyes where character and soul are revealed. I've been around horses all my life. Grew up with horses. I didn't actually own one. But I knew a kid who did. I saw that horse plenty of times.

Second race.

Never, ever, under any circumstances bet on sentimentality, superstition, color of jockey costumes or any slightly feminine things like that. Never. EVER! Unless...a horse is named after your hometown. When a horse has a name like Greenwood Cash you know darn well the universe is trying to tell you something. Jung called it synchronicity, which is stronger than coincidence. Greenwood is my hometown in Arkansas and Johnny Cash is from Arkansas too, AND, what are we trying to win here? Say it! CASH! It's just *too* strong.

I also place $10 on Halo Minx and Saratoga Love, $10 more on Alert Envoy and stroll back to the rail to watch them approach the gate.

They're in the gate. I lean forward in anticipation. Being alone at 50 doesn't bother me a bit. Kathy had changed. I lived under constant pressure to perform, become somebody, go to therapy, get a real job, go back to school and get a degree. Just because she is a Ph.D. and just because she got two books published and appeared on "Oprah" twice, well, if you think I'm going to compete with that....

Did I say "compete"? Yes, I believe I did. Is it possible that I lost her because I did not compete well? Is it possible that I projected onto her a kind of Helen of Troy mystery and perfection, seeing in her what I could not see in myself?

They're off. Boom! Here we go again as they sprint to the first turn. Saratoga Love takes the early lead. Then Greenwood Cash makes a move down the backstretch and is first going into the second turn. I'm jumping up and down like high school cheerleader. Holding my scotch, cigar in clinched teeth and racing form slapping my thigh.

"...AND DOWN THE STRETCH THEY COME...."

"Come on, Greenwood Cash! Bring! It! Home!"

They thunder down the home stretch. Whips are flying and heads are bobbing up and down and I'm screaming, "Come on Greenwood, Cash it in!"

The winner easily...Watersail. (Something about dropping down in class. What's that all about?)

Greenwood cashed out. Halo Minx, a jinx, Saratoga Love needs a manly shove, Alert Envoy, not alert enough.

I got some pizza and a scotch. I called Jane my secretary. She and Kathy were supposed to have lunch but Kathy has canceled, naturally. Too busy. While walking the streets or sitting at a bar I find myself in a never-ending inner monologue about her, carefully explaining to her what I was trying to accomplish with my life. Why we should try again and give me more time to pull off what I was trying to do. I fantasize brilliant soliloquies filled with passion, insight and logic, build elaborate arguments defending my life and work, trying to convince her that all the reading and writing would eventually pay off. I would become the human being that I always wanted to become.

"Who's that?" she asked patiently.

"Lance Alworth," I said.

"Who?"

How could she ever be convinced when I could not convince myself? She would gladly have seen me as the person I could become, if only I could.

Standing at the rail I imagine myself a Pulitzer Prize winner, rich and famous and she suddenly inviting me down to our old cabin for the weekend where we make love like the old days and she looks into my eyes with that gaze of utter respect and admiration that I saw the first time at the picnic.

I lost $30 in the third race. I lost in the fourth race after betting on a horse named Pet Brick. (You gotta go with a horse that has the nerve to call himself a Brick.)

I lit another cigar and sipped another scotch. Smoking a cigar is a man thing. You can hold it in you mouth with your lips or you can bare your teeth which makes you feel like a warrior. I've never smoked in my life but took up the habit after the divorce and after the shrink said I had a problem with masculine competition. When you smoke a cigar and hold it in your mouth with your teeth you feel like a veteran cigar smoker. Careful though if you're a novice stogie smoker. Careful if you drink and smoke and place your bets at the same time. I walked to the window and placed my felt tip pen in my teeth and placed a bet and then wondered where I put the cigar. Something hot — as in hot-hot — in my shirt pocket. "Hon, are you OK?" the clerk said laughing as I spilled the scotch, dropped the racing form and cigar to the floor.

"Fine. I'm fine." I didn't go back to that window.

OK, kid! Keep your chin up. This is fun. I don't need that stupid suburban family crap, a maid, a yard man, a lake cabin and a beautiful, successful wife. "Gimme $10 on Twila Choo Choo to win. I love the name." And the jockey's colors are green dots on yellow with blue stripes on the sleeves. Fabulous my dah-link! Riiiide him you little prissy!

A horse named Brazen Bandit, upon which I have exactly zero, bolts from the gate and immediately runs a wide lead on the first turn, hugs the outside rail down the back stretch while six lengths in the lead with what appears to be an abundance of uncontrolled energy, cuts out a calf on the far turn, runs under the grandstand and grabs a Bud Lite, and then, like that horse in the movie version of William Faulkner's *The Reivers*, when Steve McQueen holds the open can of sardines at the finish line, The Brazen One explodes like Secretariat high stepping and prancing sideways with incredible speed and confidence and, I swear it, does the freakin' moonwalk across the finish line and *wins the race!* The jockey is standing up attempting to slow him down as he flies into the first turn AGAIN! You don't suppose the Brazen Bandit's pupils are slightly dilated, do you? I mean what color was that pill?

I got another scotch and once again placed my bets. It was a fine day and I looked forward to driving to Sheridan after the races and spending the night with my brother, Dave. Big Dave, they called him in high school. All-State basketball and baseball, straight A's and voted FHA Dreambeau. There was no hurry. He and Jane, his devoted wife of 30 years, would not be home until after the passion play at the First Methodist Church, a live depiction of the Last Supper in which I was certain Big Dave would naturally be cast in the lead role as our Lord and Savior. Dave still in the role of perfection and me drunk at the track, alone, depressed, losing money I didn't have.

How did it turn out that way? Well, it started this way. Little James always trailing behind, always last, making bad grades, a Canary reader, "Can't spell his words, Wilma," trying to play ball and be a Lance Alworth. David just seemed to be a perfect kid. He was. It seemed so easy for him. Was it? Or did he struggle with his own demons as "The Chosen One," blessed beyond all others?

We've talked at length about this over the years and both agree that we are totally different in our approach to life. He has been able to accept who he is and I have struggled to accept who I am. I thought I was supposed to be like him.

Embarrassingly broke I'd have to win gas money on the exacta in the final race. So determined — desperate perhaps — was I to hit the exacta that I placed $2 bets on practically every combination among the ten horses. Chewing the wet, ragged remains of my big cigar and slightly hammered on cheap scotch I sit in the stands and await the start.

They're in the gate. Why three gates? They're off. All thirty of them. It's the Oklahoma land rush. I stumble to the rail. I have three right hands and three cigars. Then I realize I'm hopelessly intoxicated and I'm leaning over the rail amongst a few dozen other homeless derelicts and alcoholics with nothing better to do on Wednesday afternoon than drink and attempt to get something for nothing.

"Come On, Pancheeeoo!" I scream, "Bring it home you drugged up pile of Iffory soap! Don't fail me now you horse plow!"

They ran and ran and ran and ran somewhere through the trees I saw them a blur and down the back stretch in slow motion, in a deathlike silence in which I thought I heard the throaty, desperate sucking for oxygen through tiny nostrils, ...and then from above me a voice in slow motion, like he's on the wrong speed,

"AND DOOOOOOWN

THA STRETCH

THEY COME....

the competition:

"Big Dave, 33 years in one job, champion golfer (he doesn't play much any more), non-drinker (so?), non-sinner (oh, come on!) superintendent of schools, Sunday school teacher (nice), Rotary Club president (bo-ring), never divorced (lucky guy), personal friend of the President of the United States of America (I know Hillary).

"Nose to nose,"said the voice, "with...

"Kathy, Ph.D., two books published (they didn't sell), high-level consultant to corporate America (big deal), friend of CEOs (I met Elvis), personal friend of Oprah (I doubt it), successful in business (she started in my office), beautiful woman (true), perfect aunt (maybe), perfect daughter (well), perfect wife (they don't exist), perfect stepmother (ask Ryan about that), brilliant (but flawed), tender (sometimes), and drives a BMW (I've got a truck)...

"And far back, apparently in a different race, on a different track altogether...

"GJ the DJ, fired from good jobs (sometimes a compliment), never finished a degree (neither did Einstein), numerous failed projects (dare to fail grandly), many rejections (many more victories), ADD (a sign of genius?), Hermes the Twice-Divorced (yes, a flaw), drinking way too much (perhaps), gambling (Viva Las Vegas), smoking cigars (cough), chasing wild women (why not?), and in pursuit of Lance Alworth.

"BuddyGotADime?"
I looked up. The stands were empty. The horses were gone. Due to fatigue I had momentarily passed out over the railing. Just resting my eyes actually. A cold chilling wind blew losing tickets, racing forms and cigar wrappers in a dusty circle.
"BuddyGotADime," my old friend said again.
"BuyYouACuppaCoffee?" I said.
"HowAboutaBeer?" he said.
"SoundsLikeAWinner," I said.

Oh Brother, Where Art Thou?

I'm worried about my brother, David. He is apparently going through a mid-life crisis or, worse, has fallen in with lowlife hoodlums in Sheridan.

David was President of the Greenwood High School Beta Club ('61-'62), FHA Dreambeau, All-district basketball and baseball, a member of Young Republicans and voted most likely to remain calm under nuclear attack. He was a class officer graduated with honors and was unanimously selected to play the role of preacher in the youth night revival at the First Baptist Church. Dave was one of the most dependable, level-headed, solid and mature young men in the history of Greenwood schools.

After four years at Arkansas Tech where he starred in baseball and basketball, he moved on to Sheridan where he began his long and distinguished career in education and is now superintendent of schools. He's served as president of the Rotary Club, board member of the local country club, secretary of Community Home Improvement Association, founding member of the Good Parenting and Love Thy Neighbor League. He has been a Sunday School teacher at the United Methodist Church of Sheridan. Dave has always been the kind of guy you'd want your kids to look up to as a role model.

Then, the phone rang on Sunday morning. I was reading the sports page, drinking coffee, thinking about whipping up a high-cholesterol breakfast and awaiting the start of the Talladaga 500 NASCAR race. Sunday used to be a day of rest, family gatherings, Sunday dinners and then good old American football or baseball. You can have your NBA playoffs and your baseball. Give me 42 guys at 200 miles per hour bumper to bumper, doorknob to doorknob and I've got Sunday afternoon booked.

"Hello!" I said.

"Hey, James! Can you hear me?" someone screamed on the other end. "Is that you?"

"Yeah, it's me!" I yelled back. It sounded like David. But there was a thunderous roar in the phone, a combination of shouts, yelps and screams, applause, various shrieks of agony or ecstasy and something that sounded like car engines. Big car engines. I mean Chug-a-lug, glub-glub, Ka-chonka-chonka engine sounds. Deep growls like non-muffled explosions of high-octane fuel within tightly compacted metal parts creating a series of cacophonous eruptions.

"Yeah, it's me!" I yelled into the receiver. "What's all that noise? Where are you?"

I'm about thirty feet from the green flag at the Talladaga 500. Me and David Slocum and Rick Baldwin are right in the middle of 200,000 screaming idiots. We're waiting for the green flag!"

"Talladaga? Dave, you can't be in Talladaga. I should be at Talladaga and you should be at Sunday School."

"We drove all night and we're right in the middle of it. It's totally insane and the place is like a volcano. I'll hold the phone up when they start."

"OK," I screamed. "I'm watching it on TV right now!"

Dave is no spring chick. He's older than I am and he's fallen in with rednecks, ruffians and rebels. He's never been to a stock car race in his life. He's responsible, dependable, a solid citizen. We're totally opposite. He's a Dockers man and I wear Levis. He drives a Suburban, I drive an old beat-up pickup. He has a cell phone, I just yell out the window.

He's been married to the same woman for 35 years. I've been chasing some of the same women for 35 years. He's red wine, I'm scotch on the rocks.

Dave was the kind of kid who got his homework, kept his side of the room neat, never acted up in class and painted the prettiest ceramic apple in vacation Bible School.

Suddenly through the phone I hear the most blood-curdling, out-of-control, totally delirious redneck yell that I have ever heard in my life.

"Yeeeee-iiiiiiiiiii!!" he screamed as the green flag was waved and the field of 42 cars roared down the homestretch directly in front of him. I could hear the low guttural roar better over his cell phone than the high-pitched whine that comes through the TV set. "You can't believe this!!" he screamed. "It's like a tornado and everybody is going nuts. It's like three Super Bowls and two World Series rolled into one! Yeeee-iiiii!! You wouldn't even believe this!"

Never before in his life has Dave ever yelled Yeeee-iiiii. He has never been the Yeeeee-iiiii type.

"Dave. Are you OK?"

"There goes Dale Junior, Jarrett and Gordon right beside them. Here we go!! Yeeeee-iiiii!!"

I held the phone away from my ear to protect my eardrum.

Around midnight the phone rang again. "Yeeeee-iiiii!" It was the three wise men from afar. They were still yelling into the phone about the excitement of the race. They had moved 34 miles from the speedway in six hours among RVs with rebel flags, pickup trucks with gun racks and good old boys wearing caps with farm implement logos. It was a river of raging, aging testosterone. It required almost four decades in Sheridan, but it appears that the local element finally got to him. Oh, brother! Where art thou?

Me and Elvis

For years I have steadfastly refused to discuss my personal relationship with Elvis Presley, for fear that any disclosure of our friendship might be misconstrued as selfish exploitation.

However, upon this, the 50th birthday of the man who changed the world of music, the man known as "The King," the man I knew simply as a friend, I have chosen to tell the whole story.

It all began in 1961 in Russellville, Ark. I was there for a college football game and was in the Old South Restaurant for a late-night cheeseburger with some friends. Suddenly the door flew open and in walked two men in black suits and sunglasses. They scanned the room quickly, made a hand motion, and, to our utter surprise, in walked Elvis Presley.

They settled in a corner booth. The King looked so young and thin, wearing a pink shirt with black hair swept back in ducktail fashion.

We were frantic with joy. Gathering all my courage, I walked over to the corner booth and struck up a conversation with the man I admired the most in the whole world. I told him I had learned to walk like him. I showed him my lip-curl-snarl that he had made famous. I even showed him my own version of his gyrating pelvis move and was all set to do my left leg-wiggle when he said, "Yoah bo's, coma' on'a ovah, Viva La' Vega', ya know?"

Unfortunately, since Elvis didn't always speak clearly, the goons thought he said, "Kick 'is ol'boy all the way to Las Vegas."

The two goons created a real scene, but on the way out I was able to do my left leg-wiggle. Some of my friends said Elvis loved it and was laughing the whole time.

We kept in touch after that. I didn't see him all that much, but there was an unspoken connection between us. I sent cards and occasional gifts. Naturally, he didn't have time to acknowledge them. I didn't mind, though — he had a hectic schedule with concerts, movies, buying Cadillacs for complete strangers and flying 50 people to Los Angeles for chili at Chasens. I didn't push our relationship, and I believe to this day it is one of the reasons we remained friends through the years.

The next time I saw him personally was in 1976 at Graceland in Memphis. I lived in Memphis at the time and often dropped by the mansion to visit Elvis or some of the boys, usually Earl, the guard at the gate.

I'll never forget the night of the golf cart incident.

We were having this wild party at Graceland — booze, food and, yes, women — when suddenly Big E (those of us who were close friends always called him Big E) made a phone call and ordered four brand-new electric golf carts. About an hour later, his body guards, friends and beautiful women dressed in glitzy evening gowns piled into these carts and took off. I didn't actually get into one, since I happened to be chatting with Earl at the gate, but I spotted them and immediately followed the wild procession.

We went all over the place. Four carts full of the entourage and me, running along beside them. They'd play games with me, pretending to run me into oncoming traffic and such. We laughed like crazy. The King loved his little games.

Elvis and I got very close that night, and I will always look back on that evening as the highlight of our strange, and perhaps misunderstood relationship. It happened while he was careening off the hill in the churchyard adjacent to the mansion. Big E was driving a golf cart loaded with four dolls — I don't think Priscilla was along that night — and they were coming directly at me. I was waving my arms and laughing right along with them. We were having a blast.

"Hey, Big E," I shouted as they got closer and closer, "remember me? Old South Cafe, Russellville, Ark., about 1961."

Elvis Presley, King of all rock'n'roll, looked right at me, and I looked right at him. There was a moment there when I couldn't help looking directly into those big blue eyes with the cart only five feet from me coming right at me. It was in that instant, that precious second frozen in time, that we both knew that more than our destinies were about to meet. I shall never forget it. Just before the cart hit me dead center, I heard that world-renowned voice say, "We go'ah whack 'is ol'boy he'all a way ta' La' Vega."

I woke up in the hospital.

What a party that was.

We sort of drifted apart after that. You know how it is. I moved to St. Louis and got involved in a skyrocketing career of my own. As I look back, I realize now that the reason Elvis didn't write or call may have been a touch of jealousy that I eventually became as big as he did.

What wonderful memories. The man was a sensitive artist.

Happy Birthday, big guy.

I'll never forget those special moments we shared together.

The Victory Cigar

On Christmas Day, my son, Ryan, then a senior psychology major at Boston College, very much aware of his old man's propensity for worry, anxiety, sleepless nights, and over thinking, handed me my Christmas present. A box of cigars.

Nine quality cigars. "Dad, smoke one a day and enjoy."

"But, Ryan, I don't know one from another. I'm a strictly casual cigar man."

"Pops! You need this. Smoke one, take notes, savor, enjoy and report to me on the total experience."

Ryan was concerned about his old man. It had been four years since the divorce and it was obvious I had not fully recovered. Although I had attempted to put on a good front for his Christmas visit to my Palm Springs apartment where I worked on a book, he could see that I continued to struggle. He did not know how much. With great joy I accepted the Cohiba Churchill box with the nine cigars inside.

On the first day after Christmas Ryan assisted in the selection of my first smoke. As a golfer and amateur bass fisherman, I had smoked an occasional cigar, but like most beginners very seldom had the opportunity to experience a really fine smoke. Our choice for my first quality experience was a Paul Garminian, Gourmet Series. Cigar Aficionado .com reported a rating of 87: "Vegetal character and a hint of toastiness." As a beginner I knew I'd enjoy the lighter cigars at first. The Paul Garminian held a slightly sweet taste. As Ryan baked in the desert sun reading his Christmas present, the life story of Jim Morrison of the Doors (he's heavy into guitar as well as psychology), I focused on the cigar: the draw, the swirl of smoke, the taste.

After a while I moved to the grass and lay on my back with the cigar between my teeth and my hands behind my head. There was no need for conversation. No need to think.

"Sometimes I just sits and thinks and sometimes I just sits." The words of Mudcat the Blues Man came to mind. Mudcat was also the janitor at the Fort Smith Boys Club where I was a skinny basketball player at the community college. I wasn't much of a scorer, but I was the leading rebounder on the team. At 6'5" I fancied myself a serious defender and shot blocker like Bill Russell of the famed Boston Celtics. On Sunday during high school years my brother David, the star player, and my father, the high school basketball coach, watched the black and white TV as Russell led the Celtics to 11 NBA Championships on the parquet floor at Boston Gardens. Coach Red Auerbach lit a victory cigar on national television. That was the first victory cigar I'd ever seen.

Mudcat's line, "sometimes I just sits and thinks and sometimes I just sits," is amusing enough, and I recall quoting it a few times over the decades. But it's far more than just amusing. Mudcat had no way of knowing that someday his idea about "just sitting" would be known as Zen meditation. Not because Mudcat said it but because Buddha did. Zen meditation, the art of "just sitting" would save my life. But Mudcat the Blues Man didn't know that.

Lying on one's back may not be the proper way to enjoy a great cigar. For almost a half hour I allowed the sun to pour over my face, legs and feet which rested on the trunk of an olive tree.

The cigar rested comfortably between my teeth and the smoke drifted upward and away, swirling lightly toward a blue and windless desert sky.

"Ryan!"

"Yeah."

"Sometimes...I just sits and thinks."

"Dad, as far as I can tell," he chided as you'd expect a college senior to, "you just sits and thinks most of the time."

Ryan has never been totally convinced that his old man is actually a writer-mystic-storyteller in good standing with a reasonable if not spectacular career which has kept his son in dear old Boston College with all those Eastern kids whose parents are computer executives and stock brokers. Kids can be cruel at times, but it's not intentional. Before the divorce, Ryan thought it was hilarious to accuse me of being a bum. He didn't know it hurt just a tiny bit. Maybe I feared it was true. Being a writer is lonely and time consuming. From the point of view of a son or hardworking wife, it can be easily misinterpreted as a guy sitting around in his bathrobe while everyone else goes off to work.

"...and sometimes I just sits."

Ryan laughed. He knew his Christmas gift to me was a winner.

On December 27 I chose a Romeo Y Juleta, Meddalas de Oro. With a rating in *Cigar Aficionada* magazine of 85, it is reported to be "a mild cigar with good balance and an overall creamy character. A light wood finish." Sitting in the bright desert sunlight for my second setting, I turned the TV toward the patio to watch the first of a dozen bowl games leading up to the National Championship Fiesta Bowl.

I clipped the Romeo Y Juleta and lit it by rotating for an even light. Then I leaned back in the sun to watch my beloved Arkansas Razorbacks. No matter how many decades pass, how many seasons come and go, I still feel a tingle of excitement when I see a Razorback on a cardinal red helmet. Living in Palm Springs during two years of personal recuperation from the divorce, I had lost touch with the Razorbacks. I didn't know a single player and yet I would root for the Razorbacks just as if Lance Alworth himself would take the opening kickoff.

"Listen, Ryan," I quickly turned the volume up. "They're calling the Hogs! Whoo — Pig Sooiee!"

Ryan rolled his eyes like kids do. "Pop, please. You'll scare the neighbors."

"You should've seen Alworth, Ryan," I said while blowing smoke on the patio.

"Dad, I've heard you talk about Alworth all my life. What is the deal? What is this infatuation with Lance Alworth?"

I became emotional when he asked me point blank. I had never asked myself that simple question. I had never really faced it. I knew it was about my own feelings of inadequacy that someday I would have to deal with.

I had worshipped the Razorbacks and especially the legendary, near mystical hero, Lance Alworth. When Lance came to Arkansas to play in 1958, Orval Faubus was governor, and an African-American child could not enroll in a public school at Little Rock Central High. Meanwhile, some kid named Bill over in Hot Springs was blowing hot air into a saxophone.

When Lance Alworth was voted recently as the best wide receiver in the history of professional football, the kid in Hot Springs had become president and had awarded already the Little Rock Nine congressional medals. In between were Kennedy, the Beatles, Vietnam, hippies, a moon walk, and now the Internet.

"Well, he was a symbol, Ryan. Unfortunately he became a symbol of my failures. We all wanted to be a hero, to be like Lance. For me, because my father was the coach, it was even more important. A big mistake. It took a long time to deal with it."

The Romeo Y Juleta brought a sense of peace and calm. It burned even and the taste was sweet and smooth.

Time. Sometimes you just sit and think. And wonder.

Over the next few days, with each smoking of a quality cigar I noticed a deepening of the inner monologue that we often think of as "just sitting and thinking." My desire was to enter another zone, a higher plane of tranquility. I was looking for "just sitting," that state of quietness, nothingness, Nirvana. You can smoke a cigar and play golf, talk on the cell phone, bartend, fish for bass or swordfish, drive nails, drive a truck, drink fine brandy, discuss literature, art, or the Dow Jones or the NASDAQ. But I was in search of peace, a time to just sit.

We drove to Las Vegas where I smoked a Macanudo Vintage 1993, rated 88. Made in Jamaica with filler from the Dominican Republic, binder from Mexico and wrapper from the USA. Appropriate for a smoke in Las Vegas. We drove to Las Vegas so that I could personally introduce my future shrink to what has become the most interesting, stimulating, provocative, gauche, overly lavish, entertaining city in America if not the entire world. If you think Las Vegas is about rattling slot machines and neon lights, you probably haven't seen it in a while. I wanted Ryan to notice the themes being played out in Las Vegas casinos. The average visitor is too busy ga-ga-ing at the glitter to grasp the psychological and mythological currents in the air. In no other city in America is a visitor bathed in ancient themes such as Poseidon and Neptune. Roman goddesses await your arrival outside Caesar's Palace, and on the inside Venus de Milo and a replica of Michelangelo's David. The Bellagio is spectacular with a water show rivaling the best of Ancient Rome. Visitors can watch the show from Picasso's Restaurant where the master's paintings hang alongside Van Goghs and Monets.

"Ryan, what do you think?" I asked as we sat down on a bench looking across the Bellagio lake waiting for the show.

He was speechless as I lit the Macanudo.

"Unbelievable."

It's hard to impress college seniors. When a kid drops his coolness facade and sincerely with eye contact says, "Unbelievable," you know he is impressed.

I began one of my fatherly monologues that he has learned to tolerate over the years. "There is something really important going on here that very few people understand. It's not about money or entertainment. It's deeper than that and then the money and fun play a secondary role. The hero's journey, the trip to this place to conquer, to win a prize, to find the pot of gold at the end of the rainbow is genetically coded in human beings for about 300,000 years of evolution."

He pondered upon my monologue for a moment and then said dryly, "Pop, it's about money."

"That's right, but what's money really about?" I said.

I pulled on the Macanudo. We parents often answer our own questions to our kids. When you ask a life-shaping question like "...but what's money really about?" you should shut up and just sit. Enjoy your cigar.

After a while, he answered. "Well, you know, Pops. If you are going to think about evolution and the human species as a whole, money is big game. It's shelter, it's clothing...it's about staying alive."

"You've got it," I said excitedly. "It's serious business, and it's played out in fantasy as well as reality right here."

We were quiet for a while.

"How's the smoke?" he said.

"Love it. Macanudo. One of the best I've tried. They keep getting better!"

The water show exploded from the lake like a chorus of ghosty gods in perfect ballet.

"But you're sitting in the middle of the Las Vegas strip. I can tell you this one thing."

"Pop!" he said with both hands spread palms out as if he's warding off a vampire. "Please, not the famous If-I-Had-Just-One-Thing-To-Tell-You line!"

"No, that's later...I tell you this, sitting here, in this place smoking a cigar, you don't just sit...you can't help but THINK."

Back in Palm Springs I was ready for the Cohiba Churchill.

At sundown I often walk out to the golf course here at Desert Falls where I live. I take a golf club and slip over to the range where I can hit stray balls. Ryan doesn't know that we're broke. I await the publication of my book, attempt to get my life in order after the divorce that took place just four short years ago. It was right after he went off for his freshman year that my own Beatrice, my Aphrodite, the Helen of Troy of my life informed me that she cared for me a lot but was basically unhappy in nine different categories. As a psychologist, she decided to approach our relationship in a scientific manner. After eight years of marital bliss to the smartest and most beautiful woman I had ever known, out of the blue, she handed me an elaborate chart with lines and curves and numbers. In all nine categories listed, I had received a failing grade. My life came crashing down.

As a child in school I learned that your grades determine your value to the community. Later in life you are graded in other ways. My wife handed me an adult report card with nine categories. She had no way of knowing that to me, all it said was "Canary Reader."

"Only nine?" I said. "How about an even dozen ways in which I have disappointed you?"

I had already gone to therapy, started taking Prozac, stopped drinking alcohol, lost weight, stopped cussing and given up whole milk. There was nothing more I could do. I knew in that brief moment our relationship was over.

Now in Ryan's senior year the wounds are almost healed but the struggle of career, earning a living, the money thing goes on and on. Survival. There is no need for him to worry as he begins his final semester at BC. So I don't let him know the real truth. I walk to the golf course and ponder my fate...and his.

On this day I select my 1-iron and the one Cohiba included in my Christmas collection. It is rated 89 and sells for $15.

Golf and cigars go hand in glove although the true aficionada might frown on smoking a great cigar in a strong outdoor wind. The desert afternoon is calm and I light the darker Cohiba and stroll toward the trees that will hide me from the pro shop. Swinging a club with a cigar in the mouth can be tricky and is not recommended for the high handicapper. A herky-jerky golf swing with an unexpected heavy divot might cause a clinched teeth reflex and create an unsightly teeth indentation on a fine cigar. Aware that quality cigars burn a tight, even ash, I watched as the Cohiba burned very slowly and I loosened up and prepared to hit stray balls with the 1-iron. A slow easy swing, protecting my cigar, produces a solid thwack sound and the ball streaks low and fast across the range. The cigar provides "a woody taste with excellent balance. It has smooth pepper and nut component on the palate, sweet, flinty, but not on the finish."

Balance, like in a good cigar, is the key in golf. Many golfers don't realize that the true magic of the golf swing is found inside one's own center and not in those two dozen external component parts they like to talk about on TV.

Balance is to the perfect golf swing what timing and context are to comedy. It is the unseen quality that transform sex to love making, that quality that elevates rhyming words from rap to poetry. And balance is what makes a great cigar.

I walk and hit, puff the cigar and notice the ash is smooth with an even marble-like perfection. The range balls streak across the valley from the trees not totally unlike the nighttime anti-aircraft fire we are accustomed to seeing above Baghdad during occasional wars with Iraq. Ping-ping-ping and the darters flash low and straight about 240 yards.

The Cohiba is excellent for outdoor smoking with its rich texture and perfect burn. A full inch of ash hangs on the end solid as a lead pipe. As the sun disappears behind Mt. San Jacinto, I stand in awe of the desert air, the calm, the green of the golf course with sprinklers sputtering below me on the range dotted with white balls. The smoke drifts upward. I'll walk back to the condo, pour a favorite libation and put on steaks. Ryan, who just got his final grades through the online source at BC, made a 3.9. He doesn't know those are not really his final grades. Not by a long shot. No need for him to know. Life is for the young people.

Time goes by. My book on storytelling is completed and is scheduled for release in the fall by McGraw-Hill. Ryan graduated from Boston College. I scraped together enough frequent flyer miles and flew TWA to Boston. I watched from high in the football stadium as the 3,000 graduates poured onto the field. I scanned the program. I saw his name with the words beside it...*Cum Laude.* Wiping away tears I pulled out the last of the quality cigars that I had carefully saved for this occasion, a Cuban Partagas Corona, rated 92. I cut the end carefully and placed it in my mouth. I watched as the 3,000 graduates sat below. Dignitaries, faculty in brightly colored gowns from Oxford to Stanford to Harvard. Five famous citizens to be honored with doctorate degrees. The ceremony was long and there was a threat of rain. But nothing could dampen this day. I smoked my first and last victory cigar. "An excellent cigar with a beautiful oily wrapper. It is filled with sweet spice flavors like nutmeg and a strong note of cocoa beans."

I lit the victory cigar high up in the stadium, exactly 50 years after Grandma Lizzie's death. A half century in the twinkling of an eye, a quark and quiff as Joyce would say: the farm, the bus rides with my father, tender moments with my mother, balls and buckets, reading and spelling, longing for something unknown, searching for what had been lost or forgotten.

Atman, perhaps, as Wilber suggests? The higher non-dual self, walking daily, hourly, moment by moment as witness to it all. ALL. Above pairs of opposites, beyond good or bad, beyond up or down, beyond judgement, just witness it all as such, as it is, just such. I puffed on the cigar.

I could not help think about Red Auerbach, the old Boston Celtic coach who made the victory cigar an American tradition. Today the victory cigar is a mainstay for golfers, NASCAR drivers, movie stars and for fathers at their sons' graduation with honors. As I settled back to enjoy the moment, it suddenly occurred to me that one of the five recipients who would receive an honorary Doctor of Humane Letters would feel right at home with me puffing away on my victory cigar. I imagined that he might glance up my way and smile in thanks. As he was introduced, the students gave him a rousing standing ovation. I couldn't keep the smile off my face as the college President William Leahy, said, "...now it is my pleasure to confer the degree of Doctor of Humane Letters to...William 'Bill' Russell."

Sometimes you sit and think, and sometimes you just sit. Sometimes the victory is plain for all to see, and sometimes you have to wait a while. And sometimes you have to go in search of it and work long and hard to find it.

Postscript

That was the only victory cigar I ever smoked. I don't smoke. But that day I sat up there in the Boston College Stadium puffing on a big stogie and from deep within I felt the first vibrations of healing. Closure is a word way too overused these days but it's the right word actually. A sense of completion or closure began to form inside my soul.

The previous four years had been the toughest, most challenging, most tumultuous years of my adult life. Ryan's graduation at BC and my move back to Arkansas marked the beginning of the end of an important, painful but very necessary chapter, a chapter that had to happen before I could move on to more balanced and productive things. It was that essential phase in the fully developed life that might be called the final frontier, or, in the terms of the Hero's Journey, the Supreme Ordeal. It's that time in your life when you face your own demons, when you conquer Grendel only to find Grendel's monstrous mother on your doorstep.

Kathy, the Queen Bee, and I were divorced on Feb 2, 1996. From that time until 2000 I moved six times. On February 17th of that year I moved from our suburban home, my dream home, at 217 Ladue Oaks where Ryan was raised, to a lonely apartment in St. Louis, then to delightful Malibu, Calif., then on to Palm Springs and then finally to the dry air of the desert where, alone and broke, Grendel's mother was finally slain.

Then, like Beowulf who returned home to live peacefully for 50 years, I loaded my pickup truck and drove back to Arkansas. I immediately felt at home for the first time in years.

During that time of psychological upheaval my son Ryan became the anchor in my life. He was counting on his old man to help him through BC. I needed him to serve as a reminder that life is good. Watching him grow and learn and progress from young man to young maturing scholar, I felt a sense of purpose and destiny.

I arrived in Arkansas with a solid plan. I would write, publish the things I had been writing for 20 years, tell stories, continue with my speaking career, grow a garden, find a place on the lake and live a more settled and balanced existence. For the most part I have done that and feel somehow that my real work is just beginning. The wisdom one is given through trials is deep and must be passed along to younger generations who now face even more turmoil and change than I have known in my life.

Ryan is working on a Ph.D. in Industrial Organizational Psychology at Akron University, Akron, Ohio. He teaches freshman psychology and a night school course to adult students. He takes after his old man. He can tell a good story.

David is approaching retirement as Superintendent of Schools in Sheridan, Ark., and has, as you could tell in "Oh, Brother, Where Art Thou," freaked out over NASCAR and Cajun Zydico music. Go figure.

Jane lives in Tulsa where she is a top consultant in the oil bidness. Her two kids Josh and Anna are successful athletes and already far more accomplished than either of their uncles.

Mother died on October 5, 1976. Daddy died on January 6, 1977. Ryan was born on January 22 of that same year. This collection of stories is an attempt to inform him of his spiritual, psychological, emotional and cultural roots. It is just an attempt.

Appendix

1. **Where Have You Gone, Lance Alworth?:** This title story happened just as written. I wrote it following the game while sitting on the couch in Mod 6-A. After Ryan finished moving his stuff into his room I read the story to him. Then we went to dinner. I was stiff as a board.

2. **The Farm:** Grandma Elizabeth died in 1949 when I was four years old. Some of the scenes are likely from later memories of being on the farm after 1950. Oscar actually told my father that he wanted just one flower on his grave.

3. **A Short Bus Ride:** I recall wonderful moments alone with my father before I started school in 1952. I often challenged him to foot races, and he allowed me to win.

4. **Canary Reader:** Published in *"Did I Ever Tell You About The Time..."* as a story sample. This story is a staple in my oral presentations and has been told over a thousand times to tens of thousands of listeners. A woman approached me after a speech and said, "I was in Catholic school and our groups were called 'Guardian Angels, Arch Angels and Fallen Angels.'" Why do we do that to kids?

5. **Fishhook:** Published partly in *Sports Illustrated* in "One

Leg At a Time" and *"Did I Ever Tell You About the Time..."*
this story has become my signature story as a professional
speaker. Fishhook, who married Vicki Stewart of Ft. Smith
and has lived in Rogers for many years, says, "You've
made me a star." But he doesn't believe it actually
happened. Did it happen like that? Not exactly.

6. **A Once-In-A-Lifetime-Dive:** Published in *Sports
Illustrated,* June 1979 and *Reader's Digest,* October
1979, and about a dozen other magazines. This story was
my first published in a national magazine and it opened
the door to *Sports Illustrated* where 26 more stories
appeared from 1979 to 1991. I was unaware at the time
that this story contained powerful archetypal characters
and scenes, except for the snake as the intruder into the
Garden of Innocence. The story has been chopped up and
edited a dozen times. This version is the original edition
in *SI* which paid $500 for first rights. *Reader's Digest*
paid *Sports Illustrated* $10,000 for the story and *SI* sent
me $7,000. The most money I had ever seen in my life on
one check.

7. **Stan The Man Musial:** First published in *Sports
Illustrated* October 1979, the same week The Dive story
appeared in *Reader's Digest.* I was riding high.   I
interviewed Stan Musial about those 5 homeruns, and he
remembered every pitcher, every count and every pitch he
hit for a homerun.

8. **The Day We Tackled Bobby Joe Needham:** Offered to
Arkansas Times in 1978, but they turned it down. This
story was published in *Ford Times* magazine in 1983. It
soon became one of my best oral stories and seems to
read well to this day.

9. **Jazz Kittenz:** Appeared in *Ford Times* with beautiful
artwork by Jared Lee in 1982. This story is one of those
true events that you just write down like it happened. Four
seventh graders seriously getting up in front of the whole

school and trying to play kickass rock and roll is funny. Mrs. Anna B. Adams said it was the funniest thing she had seen in thirty years of teaching. Funny?! We were very serious!

10. **The Hidden Power of a Mother:** My mother changed or redirected my life when she insisted that I had some kind of talent. I was so absorbed in sports that I couldn't see other possibilities. She could. She arranged with Mrs. Ann for me to do my *Beowulf* report orally. It's not that I was wonderful or a superstar that day or that anyone else even remembers it. But I do. I loved it. I knew I had some kind of gift. I've been using it ever since in one way or the other.

11. **Opening Night:** Not much to say about this story. Never before published. Happened just about like it is written. Why did my father say that? I don't know, but he certainly did.

12. **Never Enough:** I had a pretty good year at Fort Smith Junior College and closed it out with a good game against the U of A freshmen. Elaine Gage was the first girl I fell for who didn't think I was so cute. She thought I was a little crazy. She may have been right.

13. **Thanksgiving Day Football:** This story was published in *Sports Illustrated* in 1984.

14. **World Series Tickets:** Published in *Sports Illustrated* in 1982. The editor of *SI* at the time, Gil Rogin, said it was the best "personal reminiscence" he had seen up to that time. I felt pretty good about that and realized that I had a knack for recognizing a story when it happened and for telling it in the proper way at a later time.

15. **One Leg at a Time:** Published in *Sports Illustrated* in 1984 and was the beginning of the Fishhook tale that would evolve over a period of time.

16. **Walking With Ghosts in Ione:** Published in *Sports Illustrated* in 1991. One of my favorite stories because I

fully researched it and wrote it.

17. **Queen Bee:** This story, which has never been published, is about meeting and falling head over heels in love with my future wife. After eight years of a very exciting marriage, Grendel appeared at the castle door and the relationship ended. After the divorce Grendel's mother showed up and thus began a long journey (battle) of self discovery. Battles often turn into victories.

18. **Another Thanksgiving Run:** First published in the column for the *St. Louis Globe Democrat.* My running days were long over at that time.

19. **Day at the Races:** Never published. An attempt to explore, with some humor, a particular issue in my life, my apparent aversion to head-on competition. It's not David's fault that I set him up as the perfect standard, nor is it my ex-wife's fault that I felt in competition with her. It was all in my own mind and heart, but that's where we live isn't it?

20. **Oh Brother, Where Art Thou?:** This story appeared in the Bench Warmer column in the *Greenwood Democrat* and a few other newspapers around the state.

21. **Me and Elvis:** Published in the *St. Louis Globe-Democrat* column I was writing about 1985. I had a very popular column for a few years and thought I was on my way to fame and fortune but was immediately fired after writing a hilarious column about Italian Catholics in South St. Louis. They thought it was hilarious also, but the Archbishop didn't.

22. **Victory Cigar:** Ryan has always been a big part of my life. The last few years his world kept me somewhat focused during a time of crisis in my own life. From the day we played football on the BC campus to his final graduation day was only nine months. For me it was a lifetime.

More from Grady Jim Robinson:
Tapes

Find The Victory: Two-pack audio package. Tape One contains a 50-minute speech to 2000 school principals. Lively, funny and challenging. Tape Two contains a one-hour program on the mysterious parallels between personal childhood stories such as "Fishhook" and mythological stories, particularly *Sir Gawain and the Green Knight.* Cost $20.00 plus $3.00 for shipping.

Grady Jim: Alive and Outrageous: Videotape. One-hour program of humor and insight into corporate America. Grady Jim's typical keynote speech. Funny, challenging and just slightly on the edge. $25.00 plus $3.00 shipping.

Books

InnerAxis Golf (www.InnerAxisGolf.com). Grady Jim's search for the secret of the golf swing. $15.00

"Did I Ever Tell You About the Time..." (McGraw-Hill, 2000). How to create personal stories for use in speaking. Amazon.com. ISBN 0-07-134214-1

All items and more are available at
www.GradyJim.com
Or call 501-582-5472